RT's special strengths are his insights into gospel grace, into Bible biography, and into human hearts. All these strengths come together in this shrewd, flamboyant, nourishing book. Highly recommended.

—Dr. J. I. Packer
Professor of Theology, Regent College
Vancouver, BC, Canada

To say that R. T. Kendall's *How to Forgive Ourselves—Totally* is life changing, compelling, captivating, stunning, or gripping does not adequately portray the weightiness of this book. It is destined to become a classic, and should the Lord wait to return, this book will be read decades from now. *How to Forgive Ourselves—Totally* accompanied by R. T. Kendall's *Total Forgiveness* may become the one-two punch that brings more recovery and healing to the church than any two books in recent history.

—John Paul Jackson
Streams Ministries International

How to Forgive Ourselves—Totally is a conversation between a wise pastor and a troubled person. R. T. Kendall summons the narratives of our biblical friends to speak to us about forgiving ourselves. His mature understanding of the human experience is balanced by his theological insight. His treatment of good old-fashioned guilt exposes the manufactured facsimiles that have no real sin in them and thus should be quickly defanged of their poison. Sit down for a talk about forgiving yourself. RT will be very good company.

—Dan Boone
President, Trevecca Nazarene University

Unforgiveness toward oneself is a common missing link to real freedom and happiness among believers and nonbelievers alike. *How to Forgive Ourselves—Totally* provides the connection to understanding how to be completely free from this self-imposed bondage.

—Paul Crouch
President, Trinity Broadcasting Network

I have known R. T. Kendall for more than fifty years. He was my student assistant at Trevecca Nazarene University in 1956. Our friendship bonded during those memorable days and has grown in ever-increasing measure over the years. His latest book is a sequel to *Total Forgiveness*, which has been widely read and appreciated. I would not be surprised if this present book will exceed all expectations since so many Christians battle with the problem of forgiving themselves. I believe this book will help set you free.

—WILLIAM M. GREATHOUSE
PRESIDENT EMERITUS, TREVECCA NAZARENE UNIVERSITY
GENERAL SUPERINTENDENT EMERITUS, CHURCH OF THE NAZARENE

If you liked RT's book *Total Forgiveness*, you will love this volume, its perfect sequel on forgiving ourselves. I predict an even wider reading for this one than the first. This is the rest of the story on the subject of forgiveness and will help the reader forgive more easily and live under more peace among the issues of this life. Thanks, RT, for another masterpiece.

—JACK TAYLOR
PRESIDENT, DIMENSIONS MINISTRIES
MELBOURNE, FLORIDA

R. T. Kendall has a way of writing "where so many seem to be living." I wondered how he could ever top his classic book *Total Forgiveness*. Now I wonder no more. The volume you hold in your hand has the dynamic power to set you free. Read it…now…right now…and take God at His Word by faith, and the "midnight will soon meet the morning" in your own personal experience.

—DR. O. S. HAWKINS
FORMER SENIOR PASTOR
FIRST BAPTIST CHURCH, DALLAS, TEXAS

Two things immediately struck me when I read RT's manuscript *How to Forgive Ourselves—Totally*. Textually, no thought stands alone; every concept flows logically and powerfully into the next, like nerves connecting the human system. As I continued reading, the comparison expanded, and what I learned was awesome. Failure to forgive oneself creates a blockage that cripples everything beyond that point. In effect, by refusing to forgive ourselves, we become spiritual stroke victims, paralyzed and impaired. This is nerve damage of the worst sort, and millions are needlessly affected by it. I wish I could have had the benefit of this wonderful book and shared it with my congregations over fifty years ago.

—CHARLES CARRIN
CHARLES CARRIN MINISTRIES

This book will undoubtedly be a blessing, a comfort, and a deliverance to countless readers. It has been a blessing to me. RT always writes with great sensitivity and understanding, illustrating his biblical teaching with incidents from his own personal experience.

—DR. HARRY KILBRIDE
KERYGMA MINISTRIES

As we read this book, we were flooded with revelation that healed our souls and delivered us from memories and regret that often crowded Jesus out of our thought lives. Every book that R. T. Kendall has written has been used by God to change us, but this may well be the most powerful yet as we not only have been set free from the past but also have gained hope and guidance for the future. The body of Christ needs this desperately, and we are so thankful God has chosen His faithful servant and our precious friend RT to bring it forth in his usual straightforward and vulnerable way.

—PASTORS CURRY AND BEVERLY JUNEAU
QUAIL VALLEY CHURCH, MISSOURI CITY, TEXAS

When I heard that RT was writing a book on forgiving ourselves, I was so delighted. There is a horrible tendency amongst Christians to turn everything into an exercise in obeying the law—even forgiving others! I believe the root of that is reluctance to face the painful reality of truly receiving the grace of God, standing naked and defenseless before God with nothing but His grace to cover us. In this beautiful book, RT has given to us the tools we need to truly be, in the words of Dr. Martin Luther King Jr., "Free at last! Free at last! Thank God Almighty, we are free at last." No book that you read this year is likely to have a bigger impact on your life than this one. Read it, receive it, and rejoice. Thank you, RT; this book is long overdue.

—ERIC DELVE
VICAR, ST. LUKE'S CHURCH OF ENGLAND
MAIDSTONE, KENT, ENGLAND

How to Forgive Ourselves—Totally is R. T. Kendall at his very best. This is a courageous treatment of a much-neglected topic. It is a life-changing read and destined to become a classic.

—DR. MARK STIBBE
VICAR, ST. ANDREWS CHURCH
CHORLEYWOOD, ENGLAND

Perhaps the most liberating message you will ever hear.

—ROB PARSONS
CHAIRMAN, CARE FOR THE FAMILY
GREAT BRITAIN

Most impacting book I have read in the last decade! It is a message we *all* need to hear.

J. JOHN
EVANGELIST, GREAT BRITAIN

How to
Forgive
Ourselves–
Totally

R.T. Kendall

Charisma
HOUSE
A STRANG COMPANY

Most STRANG COMMUNICATIONS BOOK GROUP products are available at special quantity discounts for bulk purchase for sales promotions, premiums, fund-raising, and educational needs. For details, write Strang Communications Book Group, 600 Rinehart Road, Lake Mary, Florida 32746, or telephone (407) 333-0600.

HOW TO FORGIVE OURSELVES—TOTALLY by R. T. Kendall
Published by Charisma House: A Strang Company
600 Rinehart Road
Lake Mary, Florida 32746
www.strangbookgroup.com

Cover Designer: Judith McKittrick; Executive Design Director: Bill Johnson
Cover photo © Alan Kearney, Getty Images; Author photo © Chris McCallister, Southern Cross Photography

Library of Congress Cataloging-in-Publication Data
Kendall, R. T.
How to forgive ourselves-totally
/ R.T. Kendall. -- 1st ed.
p. cm.
Includes bibliographical references.
ISBN 978-1-59979-173-9 (trade paper)
1. Forgiveness--Religious aspects--Christianity. 2. Forgiveness of sin. 3. Guilt--Religious aspects--Christianity. I. Title.
BV4647.F55K45 2007
234'.5--dc22

2007002286

This book was previously published as *Totally Forgiving Ourselves* by Hodder and Stoughton, ISBN 978-0340-943649, copyright © 2007.

09 10 11 12 13 — 10 9 8 7 6 5 4
Printed in the United States of America

TO MELISSA

CONTENTS

D r. R. T. Kendall, in his book *Total Forgiveness*, has told the story of the help I gave during his ministry at Westminster Chapel to totally forgive somebody who badly hurt him.

In fact, I was able to help him because the Lord took me through a similar experience some fifteen years before. A very close friend of mine (let us call him John) betrayed my trust, and I suffered immensely because of that. Some years later, a mutual friend told me, "You know, John would like to get reconciled with you." I snapped, "No way! I'll never forgive that man!"

Our mutual friend looked at me and gently said, "Look, Josif, as long as you do not forgive him, you keep him bound with a heavy chain. But look carefully: you keep one end of the chain with both your hands, and thus it enchains you, too! You are not a free man! You will become free only when you let that chain go and let John go free!"

This picture was so vivid! It hit me in the eyes, and all of a sudden I said, "I want to be free! OK, tell John I want to see him next week when he comes to our town. I want to forgive him and get reconciled with him in such a way that we become best friends again!"

We met the following week, and I got free by liberating him! Incidentally, John is still one of my closest friends today!

It was with this personal experience that I was able to insist to RT that although the other person so badly and unjustly treated him, it was he who had to forgive. I will always remember how RT protested that the other man was totally unjust and he was totally innocent in the matter. I told him the story of my chain, but he dismissed it. But I kept insisting: "You must liberate *yourself*! Forgive *him*, and *you* become a free man again!"

Well, the rest is history—the history of the author of *Total Forgiveness*!

Now I have to tell you all another story. When I was young, I stumbled on a liberal theology book, and through reading it I lost my faith. I left the seminary in Bucharest, where I was a student, and I resigned from the Hope Church in Arad, where I was a preacher. I got a job as a teacher in a public school, and for quite a few years I was away from the Lord, living a worldly life.

Then Richard Wurmbrand, the author of *Tortured for Christ*, came out of the prison, and I went to seek counsel from him. To make a long story short, he clarified all the blockage created in my mind by the liberal books, and he brought me back to faith in the Bible as the Word of God. Then I talked to another pastor, Simion Cure, who also spent many years in prison for his faith, and I told him: "Now I understand and I believe, but I look back to the years in which I was away from the Lord and I hate the kind of life I lived. I cannot forgive myself for what I have done!"

Simion shocked me with this answer: "But who are you to forgive yourself? Who gives you the authority to forgive yourself? You have to obtain the forgiveness of the Lord and make sure you have it, and then you have to go to a church and ask the church to forgive you. You see, you were a gifted preacher, a young star, and a great hope for all our churches. And when you fell, you hurt us all! Now one church has to forgive you for us all and receive you back in our fellowship!"

I was stunned! You see, the problem wasn't simply going to a church to forgive me and to receive me back in their fellowship. By that time, I was a teacher in a high school in the city of Cluj. Being received as a member of a Baptist church in that communist time meant that I would be immediately fired from my job. And I loved it!

But I wanted to be free! I started by attending church. And one day I had a vivid encounter with my Lord Jesus Christ, and He assured me that He died for *all* my sins. After that, I went to the pastor. I told him the Lord forgave me and I wanted to be forgiven by the church and to become a member of the church.

Again to cut a longer story short, I came one day in the front of the church meeting, and I simply told them: "You know that all these years I was away, and you know what kind of life I lived. I have no excuse whatsoever. I only ask you: please forgive me and receive me back in your fellowship!"

When I said that, the pastor of the church came beside me, and here is what he said:

> About twelve years ago, Brother Josif preached a sermon in another church here in Cluj. At the end of that sermon, at a special invitation, three young men decided to enter the Christian ministry, and later on all three became pastors. One of them is me! Brother Josif was my hero and my model. And when he fell, all my world collapsed. It was very difficult for me to go on when he went astray. But now, what a joy it is for me to see him coming back. Brothers and sisters, it is my great privilege to be the pastor who greets him back. With all my heart, I recommend that we give him our forgiveness and our love.

Everybody was in tears. What a joy, and what a liberation! Let me add that the following Sunday the church celebrated the Lord's Supper. It was at that Communion that I felt my restoration was complete!

Let me add that I was expecting to be fired from my job. Well, in a strange way, my public testimony triggered a chain of events that led to my departure from Romania to England, where I obtained a scholarship to study theology at Oxford University. That was God's response to my obedience and willingness to lose the job I loved as a teacher.

Let me back RT on the importance of forgiving yourself. As I look back, I believe that when I said to Simion Cure, "I cannot forgive myself," it was pride that motivated me. I wished I did not have such a black stain on my past! But let me tell you that it has been that stain that kept me humble when the Lord started to shower with blessings my ministry. I have no right to boast. I am a sinner saved by grace.

Yes, there are situations when one has to make restitution or when one has to make public confession, and there are situations when a church body has to reestablish a person.

But the most important in all this is the forgiveness of the Lord. Who are you to blame yourself after He washed you clean in His blood?

—Dr. Josif Tson
Former President of the Romanian Missionary Society

A SPECIAL WORD FROM ONE WHO'S BEEN THERE

My personal close friend R. T. Kendall has touched my life again.

When I first read his book *Total Forgiveness,* it made a profound change in my life. How I remember it! I read it *three* times!

Now in this book, *How to Forgive Ourselves—Totally,* he's taken me much deeper, with much more releasing of my inner self. Why do I say that? Because RT has hit the nail on the head. Forgiving others is often hard enough. But many times it is not nearly as difficult as *forgiving ourselves.*

St. Paul faced his failings and particularly his persecuting Jesus by killing the saints. Mine have not been like that, but I've made many mistakes, and they've haunted my very existence. No matter how close I've been to the Lord or how much I've sought to give Him my best, I find my memory working overtime thinking, "Oh, if only I had not done that!" And it hurts. It drives away my joy of valuing myself and of allowing God to have my decision making.

I saw a sign once that said, "Don't even think about parking here." One of the best-received sermons I've preached around the world, titled "Don't Park Here," has been based on the humbling but powerful word from the great apostle:

Brethren, I count not myself to have apprehended: but this one thing I do, forgetting those things which are behind, and reaching forth unto those things which are before, I press toward the mark for the prize of the high calling of God in Christ Jesus.

—PHILIPPIANS 3:13–14, KJV

I'm so glad Paul gave us these words. I've found the most self-defeating hurt in my life is that I've continued to "park" where I have no business.

RT tells us the way out of this mess we get ourselves into. I guarantee when you've read this book honestly, without holding back the truth about yourself, you will see the light into your own soul and into the Lord's sweet deliverance.

Finally, I love R. T. Kendall. This man of God has been where you are, sat where you sit, and felt what you feel. And he's seen the clouds lifting, the dawn breaking, and the light shining again.

Take *How to Forgive Ourselves—Totally* as I'm doing, and let it flow into your whole being. You'll find you will live again.

—ORAL ROBERTS
FOUNDER/CHANCELLOR, ORAL ROBERTS UNIVERSITY

I have been almost overwhelmed at the initial response from friends and readers who read the manuscript of this book. I have never had a response like it. I knew there was a need for this book, but I had no idea how great the need for such a book was.

The idea for this book began when we were at Westminster Chapel. In our darkest hour, Dr. Josif Tson, then living in Romania, said to me what nobody before had ever said: "RT, you must totally forgive them. Until you totally forgive them, you will be in chains. Release them, and you will be released." Those words changed my life and led to my books *God Meant It for Good* and *Total Forgiveness*. I can never thank God enough for that dark hour in London. It has turned out to be, literally, the best thing that ever happened to Louise and me.

In *Total Forgiveness* I did state that it is not a "total" forgiveness until we forgive ourselves, but I did not deal adequately with this. One reader, a man from California called Patrick Day, wrote me and said that he read and reread what I had said about forgiving oneself in *Total Forgiveness*, but it did not help him much. He pleaded with me to consider writing a book on "forgiving yourself—soon."

So here it is. I pray it will bless you. I have been thrilled to have two forewords to this book: one from Dr. Josif Tson, the man God used to turn me around—a staunch Evangelical; and one from Dr. Oral Roberts, probably the most famous Pentecostal-Charismatic in the entire world.

I thank my publisher and friend Stephen Strang for his encouragement, not to mention his introducing me to Dr. Oral Roberts. I thank Barbara Dycus, executive director of Product Development, for her wisdom. I also extend my thanks to Jevon Bolden, Dinah Wallace, Deborah Moss, and other members of the Charisma House team.

The list of those who have encouraged me by reading the manuscript is too long to mention here, but I must warmly thank the same old friends who always read my manuscripts before they are published, and tell me what I need to hear, not what I want to hear—J. John, Rob Parsons, Alan Bell, and Lyndon and Celia Bowring. Other friends—such as Curry and Beverly Juneau, Randy and Nancy Wall, as well as Richard and Dottie Oates—have kindly read the manuscript, and I thank them for their wisdom. Most of all, my best critic and friend, my wife, Louise, has been indispensable in helping me write this book.

I dedicated *Total Forgiveness* to our daughter, Melissa, and I am dedicating its sequel to her as well. Drawing on her academic background in psychology, Melissa has helped me so much in the writing of this book, especially with the chapters on guilt. God has blessed us with the fulfillment of the promise that God would restore the years that the locusts have eaten (Joel 2:25). Our son, TR, is happily married to Annette and lives near us, working full-time with me in my ministry. Melissa works for Daystar Television Network in Dallas, Texas.

I pray that this book will set you free and give you a future you never thought possible. I predict your past will be eclipsed by a brilliant future to the degree you forgive yourself—*totally*.

—R. T. Kendall
Key Largo, Florida
www.rtkendallministries.com

"I KNOW GOD FORGIVES ME, BUT I CANNOT FORGIVE MYSELF"

You may be aware of my book *Total Forgiveness.* I have received many letters from readers of that book. Some of them kindly wrote to thank me for the book, but others had their questions that they felt my book did not answer. The most common question that readers felt my book did not adequately deal with was the issue, "How do I forgive myself?"

There is not a pastor, vicar, church leader, psychologist, psychiatrist, or counselor who has not had to deal with the question, "How can I forgive myself?" And I know that pastors and vicars continually hear the comment, "I know God forgives me, but I cannot forgive myself."

My own problems with totally forgiving myself are rooted largely in my feeling of failure as a parent. As I wrote in my book *In Pursuit of His Glory,* if I could turn the clock back, I would have spent more time with our children. You have no idea the sense of guilt I have struggled with over this. And yet it is also what has helped me most to be sympathetic with people who have a problem forgiving themselves. Therefore Romans 8:28 (NKJV) comes into play here: "All things work together for good" to them that love God and are called according to His purpose.

Perhaps you have a problem dealing with a failure, too. Perhaps in your case it was giving up too soon and always wondering what might have been. It could have been letting people down, falling into sexual sin, having an abortion, unfaithfulness in marriage, being sentenced to prison for a crime, abusing your children, lying to your best friend, or ruining another person's career. Perhaps you injured your health through carelessness, wasted years with the wrong company, gave advice that was utterly wrong, have had to live with a strategic choice that was wrong, took the wrong job, were abused but you blame yourself, did not listen to concerned friends when you were overtaken with a sin—and consequently forfeited a ministry, lost money through lack of wisdom, did not answer the call of God on your life, or waited too long to get right with God. The list is endless.

This is the kind of subject matter the present book seeks to address.

Remember that we have not *totally* forgiven if we have not forgiven ourselves as well as those who have hurt us. All of us have been hurt by others; all of us have hurt others. In the process, most of us have in some way let ourselves down and, therefore, need to totally forgive ourselves, too.

Not to forgive ourselves totally means that the feeling of guilt will not go away. Is there anything more painful than guilt?

This book is designed to set you free and to keep you from being paralyzed by the past. If you know in your heart of hearts that you have not totally forgiven yourself, then consider that God has purposefully put this book into your hands. It is because He loves you, is on your case, knows and understands your deepest woes, and plans to bring you into a freedom that will affect the *whole* of your life—physically, emotionally, and spiritually. Let the past be past.

Totally forgiving myself has not been easy. But I've done it. So can you.

As for forgiving others, I have had an easier time forgiving those who have hurt *me* than those who have hurt my wife or two children. Although I admit that total forgiveness is the hardest thing in the world we ever have to do, there is that which is (for me) the *very* hardest, namely, totally forgiving those who have hurt any member of my family. And yet, if I am honest, there are times when I think that totally forgiving *myself* has been the hardest thing of all.

Total forgiveness is like climbing Mount Everest—few do it. However, unlike climbing Mount Everest, *anybody* can totally forgive others. But if you can picture what must be the very highest peak or plateau on the top of Mount Everest, then totally forgiving *ourselves* would be precisely *that*! It is very, very hard for some of us to do. This book will explain why.

The immediate question is, Are we dealing with a spiritual problem, or is it a psychological problem? The answer is possibly both.

But the thesis of this book will be that the problem is ultimately only dealt with as a *spiritual* issue.

I write as a pastor and theologian, not as a psychologist or psychiatrist. I will hopefully not elbow in on the territory of the professional counselors. This would be promoting myself to the level of my incompetence. I want to affirm good Christian counselors. They realize that they cannot help every person who comes to them and that many problems are best dealt with at a spiritual and theological level. They also know that totally forgiving others is often the key to emotional emancipation.

However, I will not promise that the present book will help everybody whose psychological or emotional problem is of a very severe nature. But I do think I can help some people who will follow me step-by-step at a spiritual and theological level.

The achievement of totally forgiving others has helped a lot of people with psychological, certainly spiritual, and also marital problems. I have received countless testimonies from people who have said that their marriages were saved by following the steps of total forgiveness. Some of these included people who had gone to counselors and did not get sufficient help. It is not surprising to me that some people with emotional problems, who have sought psychiatrists and psychologists, have received help merely by totally forgiving others.

I am not opposed to psychiatrists and psychologists. Neither am I opposed to Christians seeking help from such professionals. I too have received help from Christian psychologists and counselors. In *In Pursuit of His Glory* I revealed that Alan and Julia Bell were of immense help to Louise and me when we were living in London.

In May 1970, when I was the pastor of the Lauderdale Manors Baptist Church in Fort Lauderdale, Florida, my church sent me to the Narramore Christian Foundation in Rosemead, California. This organization was founded by Dr. Clyde Narramore, a Christian psychologist. Their motto is "Every person is worth understanding." The purpose of my visit to California was to help me to become a better counselor. It was a one-month counseling course. But when I got there, I found out that their method of helping pastors to be better counselors is to work on the pastors themselves. In other words, they worked on *me*. I was given some rather sophisticated psychological tests to see what my own psychological profile was. I never knew I was in such bad shape! A Christian psychologist was assigned to me. I have to tell you, the month in California changed my life.

I almost went too far. I became so enamored with psychology that I seriously considered leaving the preaching ministry and becoming a Christian psychologist. I began to read Sigmund Freud, behavior psychologist B. F. Skinner, and many others—also the existentialists. "A little learning is a dangerous thing,"[1] and I felt I had become an expert in a very short period of time! Fortunately I came to my senses and gave up the idea of making a career of psychology. But it still did me *some* good, and I am thankful for the exposure I had to this arena.

But being at the Narramore Christian Foundation had a negative fallout as well. Although it is not their fault, what I learned from them was, in some ways, what led to my feeling very, very guilty. This is possibly because I had been (rightly) forced to face my own maladies, especially as a husband and a father. It led me to guilt I had never experienced before! You don't worry about a problem you do not know about! I did not know some of my problems existed. The idea that ignorance is bliss in a sense applied to me. Being out in California, taking those tests, and getting input from competent Christian psychologists made me see—and continue to make me see—how deep my failures have been. What is worse, if only I had always put into practice since 1970 the things I had learned from Dr. Narramore! And this, as you can see, is largely where I have had to forgive myself. And I keep doing it. If an important aspect of total forgiveness is that it is a life sentence (you have to do it as long as you live), so too is forgiving ourselves.

However, this book is almost entirely spiritual and theological. It should be seen as a continuation of my book *Total Forgiveness*. I would also suggest that this present book assumes you have already totally forgiven those who have hurt you or let you down in some way. It is going to be much, much easier for you to forgive yourself when you have truly forgiven others.

A behavioral problem, speaking generally, has its origin in one of three levels: the physical, spiritual, or emotional level—and sometimes it could be all three. One of my predecessors, Dr. Martyn Lloyd-Jones, a physician by training, had an advantage over most pastors. He would sometimes take one look at a person coming into his vestry and say, "Your problem is your liver," and urge them to see a doctor. There are any number of problems that have their origin in one's physical health—whether irritability, sleeplessness, depression, or anxiety. Dr. Lloyd-Jones and I used to discuss this issue of Christian psychology and counseling. He always insisted that a person should be sure they were healthy physically. If there is a doubt, one should get a good physical examination! This is sometimes the place to begin.

The spiritual level begins with whether you are a Christian. This may not be what you expected, but it is unlikely that you can begin to forgive yourself truly if you have not first of all been forgiven of your own sins. We all need God's forgiveness of all our sins. This is why Jesus died on the cross. I will say a lot more about this later. After all, this book is theological and spiritual in nature—just as *Total Forgiveness* is. But it would be a mistake to say that *all* problems that pertain to forgiving oneself are only spiritual.

The emotional level refers largely to your ability to handle stress. Causes of inability to cope with pressure often go back to your childhood experiences and environment—your parents, relatives, enemies, and friends—as you grew up. But as I said, the psychological arena is not the domain of the present book.

It is my own view that totally forgiving ourselves is achieved mostly by *applying* good theology (put simply) and loving pastoral care. I pray with all my heart that this book will result in what you had in mind when you decided to read it.

Definition of "totally forgiving ourselves"

I must now define what I mean by *totally forgiving ourselves*. It is accepting God's forgiveness of all our past sins and failures so completely that we equally let ourselves off the hook for our pasts as God Himself has done. It also means that since I must forgive others totally, I must equally forgive myself totally. This is an example of what it means to love our neighbors as we love ourselves (Matt. 22:39).

To put it another way, Jesus commanded us not to judge others:

> Do not judge, and you will not be judged. Do not condemn, and you will not be condemned. Forgive, and you will be forgiven.
>
> —LUKE 6:37

If I am not to judge or condemn others, it follows I should not judge or condemn myself (since God promised not to condemn me). If I am to forgive others, I must also forgive myself (since God has forgiven me). If then I do judge or condemn others, I will be judged and condemned (Matt. 7:1–2). And if I don't forgive others, I forfeit the blessing of being forgiven (Matt. 6:14–15). So if I condemn myself for my past and refuse to forgive myself, I likewise forfeit the wonderful benefit that is promised to those who enjoy God's forgiveness.

Why should God require me to accept *His* forgiveness and command me to forgive *others* but close His eyes as to whether I have forgiven *myself*? He doesn't.

I'm sorry, but this matter of forgiving ourselves is not an optional extra in God's plan for us; it is something we are required to do as obedient children of our heavenly Father.

The last thing I want to do is to give you a guilt trip—if you have not forgiven yourself—at the beginning of this book! I therefore want to add that God knows our frame and remembers that we are dust (Ps. 103:14), which was the way we were formed *before* the Fall in Genesis 3. You and I were not only created with dust (Gen. 2:7) but also were born into a *fallen* state, which makes it even harder to please God and forgive ourselves as we would like.

Let me explain what I mean by "fallen" state. St. Augustine (354–430) put forward four stages of humankind that set the pace for the Christian church's doctrine of sin for hundreds of years:

1. *Posse peccare* (able to sin)—that is, Adam and Eve before the Fall in Genesis 3

2. *Non posse non peccare* (not able not to sin)—that is, the state into which all people are born after the Fall

3. *Posse non peccare* (able not to sin)—that is, those who have faith in Christ

4. *Non posse peccare* (not able to sin)—that is, once we are in heaven[2]

It is the second stage above—not able not to sin—our fallen state, into which we are all born. This is the way we all are by nature; there are no exceptions. You and I were born into a state whereby we cannot help sinning, and this condition begins at our birth and is why we came from our mother's womb speaking lies (Ps. 58:3). You don't need to teach a child how to lie; they come by it naturally. It is not until we are glorified that we will be unable to sin (Rom. 8:30). The point is, God knows our frame and remembers we are dust—even before the Fall.

Furthermore, God is so gracious. He knows and sympathizes with our struggles (Heb. 4:15). He commands us to do the Father's will but also tenderly leads us, inch by inch, day by day, to bring us to full obedience to Him. But at the same time we need to know that forgiving ourselves is a serious matter, and it is something we must do.

We will see in this book, therefore, that forgiving ourselves is not only a privilege; it is a command. It therefore follows that if I do *not* judge or condemn myself for past sins, I will not be condemned, and if I *do* forgive myself for past sins, I will enjoy God's forgiveness—as in the case of forgiving others. In the sight of God, these three requirements are equally vital:

1. Accepting God's forgiveness
2. Forgiving others
3. Forgiving ourselves

To summarize, if I judge or condemn myself, which is the same as not forgiving myself, I forfeit the blessing from God that would be mine.

And yet it is a major leap forward to do these three things. Otherwise why would Jesus promise a great reward to those who love their enemies? (See Luke 6:35.) It is because we are talking about something that is not easy to do! But the apostle Paul set the example for us. Here are some extraordinary words that some have found puzzling:

> I care very little if I am judged by you or by any human court; indeed, I do not even judge myself. My conscience is clear, but that does not make me innocent. It is the Lord who judges me.
>
> —1 CORINTHIANS 4:3–4

What Paul means is this: he is not going to let people who judge him also govern how he feels about himself. Indeed, he is not going to let their opinions bother him! He even adds, "I do not even judge myself." Think about that! He is so free from any guilt over his past that he refuses to go where God Himself has declared, as

9

it were, "No trespassing allowed"—to quote Corrie ten Boom. She used to say that this very sign is posted over our sins that have been washed by Christ's blood to keep us from trying to go into forbidden territory. So if God has forgiven Saul of Tarsus, why should Paul now question that fact by judging himself? The answer is he won't!

The thesis of this book is that God wants you to forgive yourself and that you can do it by believing what He has said in His own Word—the Bible. It is also of no small comfort to learn that the best of God's people—even the giants in Scripture—had similar problems. Some of them had a lot to answer for. They needed God's forgiveness and needed to forgive themselves, too. I hope to make forgiving yourself as easy as possible for you to do.

PART I

GUILT AND GRACE

CHAPTER I

TEN REASONS WHY WE SHOULD TOTALLY FORGIVE OURSELVES

There is no fear in love. But perfect love drives out fear, because fear has to do with punishment. The one who fears is not made perfect in love.

—1 JOHN 4:18

God does not oppress us.

—DR. MARTYN LLOYD-JONES

Have you ever felt guilty at the thought of totally forgiving yourself? I have.

The idea is this. What I have done is so horrible that I do not deserve to be set free from guilt. It would be irresponsible to forgive myself totally and not look back. I must pay for my failure. I must see that I get justice.

The same is true in forgiving others. We are afraid they will not get justice. To forgive them sets them free and therefore means they may not get punished. When my friend Josif Tson said to me,

"RT, you must totally forgive them," I was not happy. Josif recalls how angry I was at his suggestion! But I knew he was right. I eventually took his advice and was set free with a peace I had forgotten about. The old peace I knew many years before returned. It was absolutely fantastic!

But some weeks later I began to think about what I had done. I had set them free. This meant that they were totally off the hook. They would never get found out. This was not fair. People should know! They had gotten away with it! And a feeling of anger welled up inside me. The peace left. I was back to square one.

So I forgave them again. However, not by going to them! That would have been totally counterproductive. I knew they would not think they did anything wrong in the first place. It is an important rule: never tell a person you have forgiven them unless they are sincerely asking for it. Like it or not, 90 percent of the people we have to forgive probably do not think they have done anything wrong. So don't expect to sort things out with the one who has hurt you. I therefore never approached them. The total forgiveness was in my heart. That is where the peace is. When I forgave them again, the peace returned with it!

But months later I began to ponder yet again on what they had done to us. "How dare they do this! How dare they think like that! What is more, nobody will ever know. They are not getting justice—they are totally free." And—surprise, surprise—the peace vanished again.

I have to tell you, I went back and forth, back and forth, for months. The peace would come and go in direct proportion to my attitude toward those who had hurt Louise and me.

I'm sorry it took a while, but I came to a conclusion: the peace is better!

The way forward is to set such a high value on the peace you get from total forgiveness that you prefer the peace more than their being punished. Live by this rule: *peace is better than punishment.*

FURTHER CLARIFICATION REGARDING FORGIVING OURSELVES

Before we proceed, I must further clarify what the implications are when we totally forgive ourselves. It is not only letting ourselves off the hook but also setting ourselves free from any sense of punishment. This includes accepting ourselves as we are and never looking back. It is letting the past be past. The apostle Paul had on his conscience that he had persecuted, even tortured, Christians (Phil. 3:6; Acts 22:4–6; 26:10–11), but he went on to say, "One thing I do: *Forgetting what is behind* and straining toward what is ahead, I press on toward the goal to win the prize for which God has called me heavenward in Christ Jesus" (Phil. 3:13–14, emphasis added). Paul not only knew he was forgiven; he had forgiven himself.

John said that perfect love casts out fear and that "fear has to do with punishment" (1 John 4:18). The King James Version says, "Fear hath torment." This is true, of course, but that is not exactly what John actually said in 1 John 4:18. Fear, *kolasiv echei,* "has, or possesses, punishment." The person living in fear is obsessed with the idea of punishment. This means at least four things:

1. The person who lives in fear is already punished by this fear and is truly living in torment.

2. The person is in fear of being punished by God.

3. The person in fear is always punishing himself or herself.

4. The person who lives in fear always wants to punish others.

Various translations bring out some of these meanings. "If we are afraid, it is for fear of what he [God] might do to us" (TLB). "Fully-developed love expels every particle of fear, for fear always contains some of the torture of feeling guilty" (PHILLIPS). "To fear is to expect punishment" (JB).

Fear is in a sense its own punishment. In much the same way that love is its own reward, which means it is fulfilling in itself, so, too, fear is tormenting. When one lives in fear, he or she often feels they are being punished by God all the time. If that is not enough, we do it to ourselves. We beat ourselves black and blue for our past sins. If that too is not enough, we almost always take it out on others. In other words, we fear that justice isn't going to be carried out on those who have been unjust to us. We move in on God's territory, because we are fearful that they won't get what's coming to them. Never mind that God said, "It is mine to avenge" (Heb. 10:30); we get impatient with the way He seems not to avenge us. So we try to do it for Him.

All this is traceable to fear. God has not given us a spirit of fear (2 Tim. 1:7). Dr. Lloyd-Jones used to say, "God never oppresses us." When we feel oppressed, we should realize straight away that this oppression does not come from God.

So here is what we too often do: we punish ourselves for what we have done. "I deserve to feel guilty. It would be quite wrong for me to feel good. What I did was bad. I cannot live with what I have done (or should have done but didn't). I deserve some kind of punishment." In the same way, when it comes to forgiving others, we recall what they did. We say, "They deserve to feel guilty. It is quite wrong for them to feel good. What they did was bad. They deserve punishment." So we punish them—whether by telling others what they did or making sure they feel guilty over what they did.

Not forgiving ourselves, then, is often an unconscious effort to punish ourselves. We often don't realize that is what we are doing. In the same way that we get angry if others do not get the justice they deserve and we step in and punish them, so we ourselves feel that *we* are not getting the justice *we* deserve (by our regrettable past), so we punish ourselves.

We therefore punish ourselves by not forgiving ourselves. We would feel guilty if we forgave ourselves! We should not let ourselves off the hook! And the thought of *totally* forgiving ourselves would be utterly unfair! Besides, what right do I have to take authority and forgive myself? This book will answer that question.

WHY YOU SHOULD FORGIVE YOURSELF

Why should we forgive ourselves?

1. It is precisely what God wants you to do.

This is what many of us have difficulty believing. There are various reasons for this, such as a misunderstanding of the nature of God, not to mention a faulty perception of the gospel of Jesus Christ. It seems too good to be true that God would totally forgive us all our sins, because Jesus died on the cross for us.

If you are not convinced that God wants you to forgive yourself, I hope you will be convinced by the end of this book.

It is a sin against God not to forgive ourselves. Why? Because in precisely the same way that it is a sin to be bitter, to hold a grudge, and to not forgive others (Eph. 4:31–32), so it is a sin to be bitter toward ourselves, to hold a grudge against ourselves, and to not forgive ourselves. We forgive in proportion to how we love; we withhold forgiveness in proportion to how we hate. God did not create us to hate ourselves. The most natural thing in the world is to love ourselves. This was an assumption in the command that we love our neighbor as we love ourselves (Matt. 19:19).

In the meantime, consider these words of Jesus. The opening words of the Sermon on the Mount are: "Blessed are the poor in spirit, for theirs is the kingdom of heaven. Blessed are those who mourn, for they will be comforted" (Matt. 5:3–4). I am *not* saying that not forgiving yourself is always the same thing as being poor in spirit or mourning. But the spirit of tenderness from God implied in these words nonetheless is an invitation to those who feel guilty about their past. It is an invitation to look carefully at these words and see what they *do* mean.

What do they mean? Being poor in spirit means you realize that you have no bargaining power with God and you are spiritually bankrupt. If you feel this way about your sin, then take it as a hint that God wants you to be encouraged that you do acknowledge your sin but also move on. God can use your past failure to get your attention in order that you inherit the kingdom of heaven. The very thing that haunts you most could turn out to be the best thing that ever happened to you.

The next word says that those who mourn will be comforted. This mourning refers primarily to conviction of sin, and you should see your past failure as traceable to sin. Unless your problem is one of pseudoguilt, which I will deal with in the next chapter, then acknowledge your sins before the Lord. Jesus welcomes sinners (Luke 15:2). Furthermore, Jesus always reaches out to *anybody* who mourns—as in the case when He said to the widow who was burying her only son, "Don't cry" (Luke 7:13). God does not want you to punish yourself for your past. As we will see more clearly later on, God punished *Jesus* for your failure. He will not comfort you in your mourning as long as you are trying to atone for your past by punishing yourself. And what is the promise to those who mourn? "They will be comforted" (Matt. 5:4). What else could that mean in your case but having the grace to accept God's forgiveness and totally forgive yourself?

I only know that it is said of Jesus, "A bruised reed he will not break" (Matt. 12:20). That is what you are—a bruised reed. When you are bruised, you are poor in spirit. God is calling you to accept His total forgiveness, and He comforts you with grace to forgive yourself. When you are bruised, be sure that God is not going to rip you to shreds. He is not going to shame you, demoralize you, and say, "You do not feel guilty enough, you wretched creature." It gives our Lord pain that you are in misery. He is *touched*—not repelled—by your weakness (Heb. 4:15, KJV). He invites you at this moment to forgive yourself—totally.

Jesus was given a mandate to "release the oppressed" (Luke 4:18). There is nothing more oppressive than guilt. God does not oppress us and is not the author of fear. Fear is of the devil. The devil wants you to be afraid, and he certainly *does not want you to forgive yourself.* This brings us to the next reason why you should forgive yourself.

2. Satan does not want you to forgive yourself.

I have believed for a long time that one of the ways to know the will of God is to imagine what the devil would want you to do—then do the opposite. When I can surmise (and most of us have a fairly shrewd idea what the devil would want us to do) what Satan would like, I am halfway to knowing what God wants. Do the opposite of what you know the devil wants you to do, and you will be on safe territory. You need more information than that, of course; you need to know your Bible so well that you don't have to guess what God's will is (Eph. 5:17). But if you can figure out what the devil would want you to do, good; that means you should do the opposite, and you will be moving in the right direction.

For example, what do you think the devil would want you to do regarding having sex outside of marriage? Be honest! You *know* that Satan would say, "Do it. Go for it. God made you to have sexual fulfillment." The devil always wants what is against God's Word, the Bible. The Bible has made it clear that sex outside of marriage is sin. I'm sorry, but there is no gray area here. When you therefore know what the devil would want you to do regarding sex outside of marriage but you remain chaste and pure, you know you have honored God.

The devil would *not* want you to pray and read your Bible. So what should you do? You pray and read your Bible all the more! I could go on and on. But I am counting on you to know what I mean by now.

So, regarding forgiveness, what do you suppose the devil wants? In 2 Corinthians 2:10–11, Paul said, "I have forgiven in the sight of Christ for your sake, in order that Satan might not outwit us. For we are not unaware of his schemes." I love the Living Bible's translation: "A further reason for forgiveness is to keep from being outsmarted by Satan, for we know what he is trying to do" (v. 11).

Why would Paul refer to forgiveness in connection with the devil's schemes? The answer is very sobering: *because our lack of total forgiveness is an open invitation for the devil to move in.* In other words, when I do not totally forgive those who have hurt me, I have said to the devil, "Come and get me. Do what you want with me." This is scary. I certainly don't want to do that. But Satan is crafty and is lurking around us day and night, looking for an entry. When he finds us holding a grudge, he exploits it to the full. He knows that as long as I do not totally forgive, the Holy Spirit—the heavenly Dove—will fly away for a season. God cannot use me to the full when I am carrying a grudge.

So too, then, with forgiving ourselves. Satan does not want you to forgive yourself. He loves your misery. Your bondage makes him happy. You are no threat to him or his interests when you are punishing yourself, fearing God's wrath, and living in torment over what happened yesterday—or years ago. By the way, the devil knows what happened in your past, too. He has been around for thousands of years and got on your case the moment you sided with his archenemy Jesus Christ. He will exploit your past to the hilt. His design is to keep you paralyzed and living in a pit of near despair over what is in the past.

Would you not agree then that a good reason to forgive yourself is because it is the opposite of what the devil wants for you? Since you know that what he wants is for you not to forgive yourself, then do the opposite. I pray that in this moment you will begin to forgive yourself—totally.

3. You will have inner peace and freedom from the bondage of guilt.

There is nothing to compare with the peace and freedom that comes from total forgiveness. "Where the Spirit of the Lord is, there is freedom" (2 Cor. 3:17).

I have told many times about the Damascus road experience I had while driving in my car on October 31, 1955. It was not my conversion, however; it came a few years after my conversion. My point in mentioning this is that I was given the most wonderful peace, joy, rest of soul, and assurance on that day. It was incredibly brilliant. But about ten months later, for some reason I lost the peace I had. I tried every way under the sun to get it back. I started praying for two hours every morning (like John Wesley). It did me no harm, but I didn't get the peace back. I started tithing. It did me no harm, but I didn't get the peace back. I started double tithing (for a while). It did me no harm, but I didn't get the peace back. I would ask any godly person to lay hands on me for a greater anointing. All these things no doubt helped me in my spiritual growth.

But when I took Josif Tson's words seriously, applying them by totally forgiving those who hurt me, I was amazed! The old peace returned!

God will do this for you, too. He is no respecter of persons. He beckons you as you read these lines to enjoy total forgiveness.

That includes forgiving yourself.

You will perhaps ask whether I have had an equivalent experience in totally forgiving myself as I did in forgiving others. The answer is yes, but it was not an exact equivalent experience. But almost. The peace that came to me from forgiving myself—being set free from guilt over being a father that was too busy—came in waves and stages. It has not been so dramatic, but it has been equally satisfying. And, believe me, this satisfaction has been just as important and fulfilling as the peace that came to me from forgiving others. I say that because the enormity of the guilt I felt was so awful that I needed help! God brought me through this. Otherwise I could not write this book.

You too should forgive yourself because of the peace and freedom that awaits you. Nobody knows better than I how it feels when the devil reminds you of your past and your shortcomings. The feeling is horrible.

Are you weighted down with guilt over the past? It does not need to last. I am hoping that in these lines you are moving toward the internal victory and peace that awaits you. There is light at the end of the tunnel! Your emancipation could come one of two ways: either you could have a sudden experience by the grace of the Holy Spirit that sets you free, or you may, like myself, come into this in increments. Either way is just as valid, for when you realize you have forgiven yourself, the result is inner peace.

4. The degree to which you forgive yourself may directly relate to your usefulness.

When I find myself wallowing in self-pity, I am of little use to do my work. Not forgiving myself is paralyzing.

This is the way it was with King David. We will take a closer look at him later, but I am referring now to how he grieved over his son Absalom's tragic death. David knew all too well that what happened to his son actually began with David's own sin and folly. But his mourning for Absalom went too far, and he almost had another crisis on his hands. His servant Joab warned him to snap out of this grief and self-pity at once or his followers would desert him. David immediately took Joab's advice (2 Sam. 19:1–8). Not forgiving yourself is immobilizing. It diminishes your usefulness.

Most of my ministry has been preparing sermons and preaching. It is impossible to say which I enjoy more—preaching or preparation. But with either of these, I am utterly dependent upon the anointing of the Spirit. If the anointing is there, preparation comes easily. So too with the preaching. But the absence of the anointing means that I can struggle for hours and days in preparation. Why? No insights come. I live for insight; that is my calling. But insight comes in direct proportion to the anointing, and the anointing comes in direct proportion to my relationship with the Holy Spirit.

In a word, when I grieve the Holy Spirit, insights are nowhere around. My own style has been not to read commentaries and books in preparation unless I am completely confused; then I turn to others. What thrills me most of all is when the Spirit enables me to see things in the Bible without the aid of other writers. When the anointing is on me in preparation, insights come. When the anointing lifts, I might as well try to fly to the moon.

Therefore when I am preoccupied with my failures of the past, I lose heart. I cannot get anywhere in preparing a sermon or writing a book. I am helpless. Therefore I have learned that it is in my own interest to forgive myself totally and not listen to Satan's accusations! The only way forward for me has been to disregard every single suggestion of the devil that would bring me down! In other words, I can tell you that totally forgiving others and totally forgiving myself have been my lifelines to the anointing of the Spirit.

Whatever your own gift and calling is, I daresay you are in the same situation. You will struggle in your life and calling when you are weighted down with guilt. Guilt and usefulness do not get on well with each other! Therefore I would urge you to accept the thesis of this book if only for this reason: your usefulness will be impaired as long as you are crippled internally by guilt from your past. Do not deprive the Holy Spirit of the pleasure He gets by using you to the full!

I knew a doctor in Florida who drank heavily in order to work through the pain of his past. What was so sad was that he would leave his patients waiting. He would get drunk and not be able to come to work. He eventually lost his practice. This is perhaps an extreme example of how guilt keeps one from being useful, but let me caution you, should you need it: alcohol will not make the past go away. Totally forgiving yourself must be done soberly, consciously, and voluntarily. Just as in the case of forgiving others, totally forgiving yourself is an act of the will. But it leads to your being at your best.

5. Totally forgiving yourself will help you love people more.

The reason you do not forgive yourself totally is very possibly because you do not like yourself. Some people think it is an admirable thing to say, "I hate myself." I must lovingly tell you, that is an abominable thing to say. Do you honestly think that God wants you to hate yourself? Do you think He made you to hate yourself? Why ever did our heavenly Father tell us that we should love God with all our hearts but also to love our neighbors *as we do ourselves* (Matt. 19:19)? I must say it again: these words carry with them an implicit assumption that we love ourselves. It is normal to love yourself. You were created that way. It is sin that brings about self-hatred.

People who do not totally forgive those who hurt them often do not like themselves. It is not surprising, then, that they struggle with liking people. So too with forgiving yourself. When you totally forgive yourself, your perception not only of yourself but also of others changes. They aren't so bad after all! What is more, you begin more and more to care for others—and to love them.

The fringe benefits that come from forgiving yourself are vast. And one of them is that you find it easier to love people. I do not say that forgiving yourself will make you a Mother Teresa, but you may well be surprised how much easier it is to get involved in other people's problems and worries. But when you and I are so preoccupied with ourselves, we somehow never get around to caring for others, much less loving them. Forgiving ourselves is emancipating. You begin to love yourself as God intends, and you find it easier to care for others.

Neither does this mean that you will become an extrovert. You can in any case be an extrovert and not care about others. But there is an inner freeing of oneself that enables you to be concerned about other people. We are not speaking therefore of a personality change, but I am saying that forgiving yourself will enable you to stop focusing only on yourself and to focus also on others. You are never ever asked not to care about your own needs. What Paul said is this: "Each of you should look not only to your own interests, but *also* to the interests of others" (Phil. 2:4, emphasis added). It was at that point Paul embarked upon one of the most sublime passages in all Holy Writ, which was all about becoming more like Jesus (Phil. 2:5–11).

Jesus did not hate Himself. He was sinless, of course, and we are not expected to become entirely like Him in this life. (That awaits our glorification. See 1 John 3:3.) But I am saying that totally forgiving ourselves will help us to love people more than before. For when we have not forgiven ourselves, we are not in a position even to think about loving others, because we are consumed with ourselves.

6. People will like you more when you have forgiven yourself.

Of course you want to be liked! The person who says, "I don't care what they think," when it comes to the human need of affirmation almost certainly has a severe personality handicap. We all want to be liked. It is human to want friends. Dale Carnegie wrote a best seller that sold millions—his book *How to Win Friends and Influence People.* So much of what he taught is embedded in the Book of Proverbs. He was quite biblical without knowing it. But you can read that book, and even profit from it, and find that it may not make people like you—when you are riddled with guilt. The thing is, when you totally forgive others and yourself, much of what Dale Carnegie taught might be exemplified in you without your having read his book!

"A man that hath friends must shew himself friendly" (Prov. 18:24, KJV). Do you want people to like you? Be friendly! But it is so hard to do this when we are bedeviled with our own personal problems.

When I was a pastor in Fort Lauderdale, a lady came to our church who said that our people were so unfriendly. I alerted some of the members there and urged them to go out of their way to be nice to this lady. They tried but noticed that she always left the service during the last hymn and went and sat in her car all by herself until her husband came out. She never gave the people a chance! The problem was, she was consumed with herself.

I don't mean to be unfair, but not forgiving yourself is a selfish thing. I'm sorry, but it is. It is an exhibition of the wrong kind of self-love. There is a difference between loving yourself and self-love. It is not a play on words. Self-love is preoccupation with your personal desires and concerns; loving yourself is respecting yourself as God intends.

In a word, forgiving yourself makes you more likeable. People will want to be near you. They will feel that you care about them.

My friend Lyndon Bowring has more close friends than anybody I have ever met. I know a dozen (I am one of them) who regard him as their best friend. Why? I happen to know. Lyndon is one of the few persons I have become acquainted with who doesn't focus on himself but on those who seek him out. Everybody seems to want to be near him. He not only tolerates listening to people, but he also loves them! And they love him.

The place to begin, if you have a problem with people not liking you, is to forgive yourself—totally.

7. It will enable you to fulfill all God has in mind for you and thus keep you from being paralyzed by the past.

The gifts and calling of God are without repentance, which means that they are "irrevocable" (Rom. 11:29). You cannot lose them. Even King Saul, in his disobedience and pursuit of David (hoping to kill him), still prophesied with the same gift God gave him some time before (1 Sam. 10:9–11; 1 Sam. 19:23–24). This is proof enough that having certain gifts, however beneficial, does not require us to walk with the Lord.

Paul refers to various gifts of the Spirit in 1 Corinthians 12:8–10. He then discusses different levels of service and profile one may have in the church as being the foot, the hand, the eye, the ear, and so on (1 Cor. 12:14–29). But he shows that these gifts are worthless to the body of Christ if we do not have love (1 Cor. 13). Part of love is not pointing the finger; in other words, keeping no record of wrongs (1 Cor. 13:5).

Forgiving yourself is refusing to point the finger at yourself in a way that keeps you feeling guilty. Love keeps no record of other people's wrongs, and, when forgiving ourselves, it keeps no record of our own wrongs. Not that we can ever forget our past—no. Neither do we forget what others have done to us; it is just that we do not bring these things up. So in the same way, we must not bring things up to ourselves. We refuse to think about them, refuse to dwell on them.

When you have totally forgiven yourself, it brings considerable confidence. Consider Simon Peter. He denied that he even knew Jesus to a Galilean servant girl. This is because the authorities were watching. Peter was in utter fear before them. But when the rooster crowed and Jesus looked at him, Peter knew he was found out and wept bitterly (Matt. 26:69–75). Some seven weeks later Peter addressed thousands on the Day of Pentecost with a fearlessness and confidence that baffled everyone (Acts 2). How was this possible? Peter was totally forgiven and totally forgave himself.

When we cannot forgive ourselves it is hard to look at people in the eyes. It is hard not to look down. We feel guilty and look guilty.

God wants to use those who are free of guilt—totally forgiven. But that forgiveness is of little value to our psychological frame when we do not truly *believe* we have been forgiven. When we truly believe we have been forgiven, it shows. When we have totally forgiven ourselves, it shows. God can use us. People will want what we have.

8. Your own physical health could be at stake.

In *Total Forgiveness* I referred to non-Christian organizations on both sides of the Atlantic that have been set up to help people to forgive. They are not doing it with the teachings of the Bible in mind. They are doing it for other reasons: one's health and well-being.

It has been proven by medical research that holding a grudge can injure your health. Studies have revealed that unforgiveness can lead to high blood pressure, heart disease, kidney disease, arthritis, and other ailments. I don't want *you* to think that if you have any of these problems, this is the reason. But with some people this is the case.

So if non-Christian organizations can be formed to help people overcome grudges without using the Bible, surely those who believe the Bible should take the lead!

It is reasonable to assume then that if anger and bitterness are injurious to your physical health, not forgiving yourself is bad for your health, too. This is because you are holding a grudge against yourself!

In the Lord's Prayer, Jesus put our physical needs before the spiritual. First came "give us this day our daily bread"; then came "forgive us our trespasses as we forgive those who trespassed against us." (See Matt. 6:9–13; Luke 11:2–4.) Why did Jesus put the physical before the spiritual? It is because we have to eat in order to live. God gave us bodies. He is looking after us in the Lord's Prayer. Furthermore, our daily bread does not only mean food; it means the essentials of life—shelter and clothing—as well.

This means God cares about our health. We must take care of our bodies. They are temples of the Holy Spirit (1 Cor. 6:19). When forgiving ourselves is related to our health, that is a fairly substantial reason to take this matter seriously!

9. Your mental and emotional health could be at stake.

The main problem all counselors face—whether their clients have a religious background or not—is that of *guilt*. Guilt may well be a theological matter, but it is a psychological one as well. There is not a psychiatrist or psychologist on the planet who does not deal with this in their sessions every day.

Guilt is crippling, affecting not only our bodies but also our minds and emotions. The degree to which we cope with guilt will be the degree to which we have good mental health. Dr. Frederick Perls, who was a humanistic psychologist, used to say that he could heal any psychopathology in one hour if he could get his client not to feel guilty.

Sometimes people in the world scoff at us in the church when we behave like neurotics and not solidly mature men and women. Where we currently attend church, the pastor Steve Vetter has put this word in his weekly bulletin: "The Key Largo Baptist Church family is a group of imperfect people who have been brought together by the grace of God to worship Him." This is very true and helpful. We should nonetheless make every effort to deal with bad habits, wrong attitudes, and even emotional problems that militate against a good Christian testimony. It pleases God for His people to have good mental health. Forgiving ourselves is a good place to begin.

10. You should forgive yourself because your spiritual state is at stake.

There is an inseparable connection between our spiritual health and a good relationship with the Holy Spirit. The Holy Spirit is *in* every Christian (Rom. 8:9), but not necessarily *ungrieved* in every Christian.

The Holy Spirit is a Person—a very sensitive Person at that. He can be grieved: "Do not grieve the Holy Spirit of God, with whom you were sealed for the day of redemption" (Eph. 4:30). The word *grieve* comes from a Greek word that can mean to get your feelings hurt. The Holy Spirit can get His feelings hurt! How? By our bitterness and grudges. The next thing Paul said was, "Get rid of all bitterness, rage and anger, brawling and slander, along with every form of malice. Be kind and compassionate to one another, forgiving each other, just as in Christ God forgave you" (Eph. 4:31–32).

When we are filled with anger and bitterness, the Holy Spirit is grieved. This does not mean we have lost our salvation. Paul said we are "sealed for the day of redemption"—nothing can be clearer than that! But when the Spirit is grieved, as when the heavenly Dove lifts from us, we are left to ourselves. It is because of a temporary lifting of the anointing of the Holy Spirit. The result is that we are irritable, have no presence of mind, cannot think clearly, and have little or no insight as to the next step forward.

It all comes down to this matter of total forgiveness.

Therefore we must totally forgive ourselves if we want the heavenly Dove to rest on us—and if we want to enjoy the fruit of the Spirit such as love, joy, peace, longsuffering, gentleness, and so on. (See Galatians 5:22–23.) Forgiving ourselves helps ensure that the anointing is on us; not doing so means that we forfeit a measure of His presence.

Temporarily losing a sense of God's presence does not need to happen. It should not happen. But it does happen. I have grieved the Spirit so many times that I would die a thousand deaths if you could see a video replay of my whole life. But you won't, because God has forgiven my sins. The blood of Jesus has washed them all away. And the least I can do, therefore, in the light of God forgiving me, is to forgive myself.

That is what He wants of you and me. Totally forgiving ourselves is not merely an option; we have a command from God to do this. With this mandate accepted by us, God can use us to exceed all we ever dreamed of.

He will use *you* to an extent you never thought possible. If God can forgive and use a man who knew Jesus as intimately as Peter did and who fell pitifully and horribly, He can use you and me. Jesus never stopped loving Peter. Knowing in advance that Peter would deny Him, Jesus even said to him, "I have prayed for you, Simon, that your faith may not fail. And when you have turned back, strengthen your brothers" (Luke 22:32).

Peter had Jesus's prayers behind him. So do we. Jesus's prayer for Peter enabled him to forgive himself. His prayer will do that for you, too.

CHAPTER 2

FALSE GUILT

You have to look people in the eye and make them feel guilty.

—A THIRTEEN-YEAR-OLD GIRL SCOUT
ON HOW SHE SOLD 11,200 BOXES OF COOKIES

Cast all your anxiety on him because he cares for you.

—1 PETER 5:7

A guilty conscience is the seasoning of our daily life.

—PAUL TOURNIER[1]

The nice thing about being a celebrity is that when you bore people, they think it's their fault.

—DR. HENRY KISSINGER[2]

False guilt is a sense of shame in our hearts that God did not put there. It is sometimes called pseudoguilt. Freud, for example, taught that pseudoguilt is an unconscious need for self-punishment, self-torment, or self-sabotage. This is the sort of thing we sometimes can do. One can accept an element of truth even from one whose system you would not totally endorse. The word *pseudoguilt* comes from the Greek word *pseudos,* which means "untrue" or "lie." It is false as opposed to *true,* not false as opposed to *real.* For false guilt is real. It is painful. It can be torture. But if we can *recognize* and *identify* false guilt for being precisely that which did *not* come from God, as Christians we are often on our way to being set free.

The bottom line of this chapter is that we should learn not to feel guilty once we see that it is pseudoguilt at work. Do not be controlled by false guilt.

One way forward in forgiving ourselves therefore can be summarized: we should not let ourselves be worried by any guilty feeling that is not from God. In the next chapter I will deal in detail with true guilt. In the meantime, here are two principles:

1. You must learn to identify and dignify what is from God (true guilt).

2. You must learn to detect and reject what is not from God (pseudoguilt or false guilt).

If you apply these two principles, you are well on your way to forgiving yourself and letting yourself totally off the hook.

God does not want us to give any time or respect to what is not from Him. It is part of His jealous nature. (See Exodus 34:14.) He is jealous of anything that grips us to the degree it diverts our attention away from Him. Pseudoguilt is never from God. He absolutely does not want you to be controlled by it.

And yet it is not a sin to have false guilt. We all experience false guilt, perhaps several times a day. But it becomes a sin if we know it is pseudoguilt that is driving us—and then we persist in it. When we are driven by pseudoguilt, we are—even if unwittingly— dignifying the flesh and the devil and not the Spirit of God.

Pseudoguilt has its origin in the flesh. The flesh is the sinful part of the soul. We are all born with it and have to contend with it until we die. It is what wars against the Spirit (Gal. 5:17). By nature it seeks what is evil, not good (Rom. 3:10–18). According to John 6:63, the flesh "profiteth nothing" (KJV), "counts for nothing" (NIV), "has nothing to offer" (JB), "is of no avail" (NEB), and "will not help you" (PHILLIPS). The flesh is, speaking generally, that natural weakness in all of us that is fertile soil for pseudoguilt.

The salvation that is offered in Jesus Christ is for the whole person (1 Thess. 5:23), but it is not obtained all at once. Salvation is promised to us in basically two stages:

1. Conversion, being born again (John 3:3)
2. Glorification (Rom. 8:30)

It is not our conversion but our glorification that makes us perfect. When we are glorified—which takes place when we see Jesus face-to-face—we shall be like Him and will no longer be weighted down by sin (1 John 3:3). But until we are glorified, we all struggle with the flesh—and also the devil. The time between conversion and glorification is called sanctification. It is the gradual process by which we are made holy. Our sanctification happens in degrees.

Nobody is perfect in this life—in mind, emotions, soul, heart, or body. Nobody is perfectly sanctified in this life. Not only that; some people grow faster than others. At the natural level, some people develop more rapidly than others—physically and mentally. So at the spiritual level, some grow in grace more quickly than others. There are many reasons for this, among which are our heredity and environment. Not all Christians have the same aptitude for biblical things, and not all have the same background or childhood experiences—a matter that is not unrelated to our spiritual growth.

I believe that the human personality is like an iceberg—you see only a small portion of it. Most of it (probably 90 percent) is submerged in water and never seen. When we see each other, we see only "tips" of icebergs. We cannot see what is underneath and what motivates a person to be like they are. Furthermore, it is a grave mistake to assume that all people, when they are converted, should grow at the same rate. God could heal the body when He saves the soul, but He usually doesn't. Conversion does not change our body chemistry or erase injured emotions that have set in from the past. If a person is diabetic prior to conversion, they will still have to take insulin afterward. If a person is phlegmatic or melancholy before they are saved, they don't become sanguine and outgoing when they are saved. If a person had difficulty with algebra before conversion, they will have difficulty with it afterward. So if a person has emotional problems before they come to Christ, you can expect they will have emotional problems after they are in Christ. The blood of Christ washes away our guilty past, yes; but that blood does not eradicate the fleshly nature, the memories, or the damaged emotions. These memories and damaged emotions are embedded in the iceberg that has been submerged in the sea.

This is partly the reason why some Christians grow in grace more rapidly than others. It is why some take to theology or Bible study more easily than others and even manifest the fruit of the Spirit more quickly than others. Although there are testimonies of people who have overcome severe emotional handicaps when they were converted and surprised everybody by their maturity, not all are like that. Every person is worth understanding, and the Christian faith is designed to relate to the whole person. Just remember, then, that not all believers grow in the same length of time or in the same manner as other Christians. Likewise, neither do emotional problems go away just because a person has been given faith in Christ.

We all have damaged emotions that stem from childhood. Nobody who has ever lived had perfect parents or a perfect environment. As a consequence of an imperfect psychological blueprint, we are vulnerable to a sense of shame that is not from God but which at the same time seems as natural to us as a bird flying in the air or fish swimming in the sea. Whether we are driven by a sense of inferiority, unrestrained ambition, or unattainable perfection, we are all likewise vulnerable to pseudoguilt as long as we live.

False guilt should at times be identified as counterfeit guilt since it often comes directly from our great accuser—the devil. Sadly, most psychologists do not have a place for the devil in their counseling. But, as I will stress later in more detail, the devil is alive and real and will make a constant effort to exploit our pseudoguilt. The devil therefore gives us counterfeit guilt. False guilt and counterfeit guilt are in a sense the same, but I make a distinction, because Satan, when exploiting our pseudoguilt, will put ideas in our heads that we may truly believe are from the Holy Spirit (2 Cor. 11:14). The devil always exploits the flesh. He is "a liar and the father of lies," said Jesus (John 8:44), and he is the expert in making us feel guilty by always accusing us (Rev. 12:10). Counterfeit guilt should be recognized as such as soon as possible, then refused and resisted. We must never be governed by what the devil has put into our heads. We should be concerned about true guilt, which pertains to our relationship with God and what He thinks.

False guilt therefore has basically one of two origins: the flesh or the devil. Pseudoguilt, I must keep repeating, is never from God. In this book I hope to show how to recognize it and overcome it—not to a level of perfection, but nonetheless to a life that is generally victorious over pseudoguilt. In a word, forgiving ourselves.

Never forget that the devil will take full advantage of our flesh and will exploit our weaknesses to the hilt.

Pseudoguilt therefore is not only real but can be very powerful indeed. Though it is false, or counterfeit, it is potentially very damaging. Believe it or not, false guilt is frequently more real to us than true guilt. Whereas we should be concerned about sin against God, from which arises genuine guilt, it is often pseudoguilt that distracts us. Pseudoguilt may make us feel "guiltier" than true guilt does. In other words, when it should be true guilt that ought to grip us, it is frequently the other way around; what gets our attention so often is that which does not have its origin in God.

To summarize what I have said so far: when I refer to pseudoguilt or false guilt, I am not saying that such guilt does not exist. It not only exists, but it is also often the main problem many Christians face when it comes to forgiving themselves. "I know God forgives me, but I cannot forgive myself" almost always refers not to true guilt but to pseudoguilt. And yet the irony is, as I said, false guilt becomes true guilt when we persist in not forgiving ourselves. In other words, if not dealt with, false guilt becomes sinful and hence true guilt before God. For it is a sin not to forgive ourselves.

As I will show in detail later, true guilt exists when we feel a valid sense of shame for having sinned against God and having not depended upon the blood of Christ for the forgiveness of our sins. What is more, true guilt is there when we have sinned, whether we feel it or not. In a word, God may regard us guilty in His own eyes without our necessarily feeling any sense of shame for our sin.

And yet, strange as it may seem, we can have pseudoguilt toward God. This is because we can feel we have let Him down when in fact we haven't at all. It happens, for example, when we live by a standard He never had in mind for us. We can imagine He is demanding something of us when He is not—like not meeting a requirement that He never put to us in the first place. I am sure that many, many Christians have this kind of guilt. It often happens in church work. They charge themselves with letting God down for not doing this or not doing that, when in fact God may never have required such activities.

Pseudoguilt also exists when we feel a sense of shame for having let people down. This too can eventually become true guilt before God. We are not required by Him to become beholden to people. In this case, then, pseudoguilt becomes true guilt because we are preoccupied with what people think. Pseudoguilt can be defined as not meeting the expectations of others, imagined or real. But it can become true guilt even if we don't feel a sense of shame toward God. As I said, true guilt may exist and we don't feel "guilty." But when pseudoguilt rises up in our hearts, we so often feel guilty.

It should not be surprising, then, that pseudoguilt exists when we feel we have let ourselves down. This too is because we have imposed a standard for ourselves that may have been unrealistic. I may set a standard that I write a certain amount of words each day on a book, and if I don't come up to that standard I feel guilty. A child may feel guilty because he or she doesn't make the grades the parents expected of them. A minister may feel guilty because his congregation is not growing, or if he did not preach a good sermon last Sunday. Such pseudoguilt can still become true guilt if we become preoccupied with our performance and neglect what matters most to God, namely, trust in Him.

Reading this chapter could give you pseudoguilt! Or perhaps true guilt! This is because it could make you feel guilty that you feel so much guilt all the time, and then this in turn becomes guilt before God.

Let me put your mind at ease. We are all in the same boat. A trick of the devil is to isolate us and make us feel our problem is unique and that we are the only ones who feel like this, that nobody is as bad as we are. A sense of guilt, true or false, is inevitable in this life. As for true guilt, we are all sinners. As for pseudoguilt, we are all human beings.

General Examples of False Guilt

Let me give some examples of false guilt:

- I pay a friend a visit, feeling guilty for not seeing him for a while; then when I am ready to leave, he says, "Leaving so soon?" And now I feel worse for visiting him.

- We chose to live in Key Largo, Florida, where I could do a lot of fishing in retirement, but I am so busy preaching, traveling, and writing that I have little time for fishing—and feel guilty for not using the boat that was given to me.

- I feel guilty for saying no to a preaching invitation (when the church felt "led" to invite me), but I feel guilty when I say yes because it will mean more time away from home.

- I feel guilty for declining to write a foreword for a person who needs a recommendation, but I feel worse when I accept the assignment but cannot give an endorsement of the book after all.

- A person says they saw me look at them, but I did not speak to them (when I don't remember seeing them at all).

- I sleep poorly but must get work done on a book. The truth is my mind is so tired that the whole day passes, and I do not write one sentence.

- I try to cut off a phone conversation—"I must let you go"—then they say, "Oh no, I have plenty of time; you are not bothering me."

- I eat in an expensive restaurant, and then I feel guilty for spending so much money.

- I order two newspapers to come to me, and then I feel guilty that neither gets read.

- When preaching in St. Andrews, Scotland, I was offered the very rare opportunity to play on the famous golf course there—the most famous in the world and to which people come from all over the world for the privilege of playing on if they are lucky enough to be invited. I chose to go fishing, because I am not good at golf. But I sometimes feel guilty about my decision, especially since some of my friends think I committed the "unpardonable sin"!

- I buy an expensive jacket at a reduced price and then feel guilty that I don't like it after I have worn it.

- When my wife, Louise, was growing up, her mother would scold her for reading so much—all very serious stuff, including Shakespeare—and called her a "houseplant" and would order her to get outside and "do something." To this very day, Louise feels guilty if she spends much time at all reading!

In other words, a feeling of guilt need not have sin at the core at all. We may regret bad judgment, poor management of our time and money, not choosing the best holiday plan, not going to the doctor soon enough, not being present when someone needed us, not making a wise investment, or even missing a plane or train when it was due to being held up by a traffic accident. We need a special grace *utterly to forget* such happenings.

REPRESSION

Pseudoguilt produces attitudes and manifestations in us that are not very becoming. This is often because we repress what we feel. Repression is a defense mechanism—a denial, sometimes done unconsciously, of how we *really* feel. "I must not dislike this person," we say to ourselves, so we tell ourselves that we *do* like this person. "It would not be a very 'Christian' thing not to like this or that person," we say to ourselves.

A friend came to see me with this kind of problem. "After all, I am supposed to be an example," he said to me. "I am a Christian leader. People look up to me. I must put out of my mind any thought that I do not like this person. So I tell myself that I certainly do like them." The result is, however, that we compensate for the guilt that is repressed. Some psychologists call this "reaction formation." We go out of our way to show that we do like this person.

For example, if we find that we don't particularly like someone and feel guilty (since everybody else apparently likes them), we compensate with this person by being overly nice or friendly. We may even make promises to them that are ridiculous: "We must get together soon," "Please phone me," and "I really enjoy your company." Pseudoguilt can get us to do silly things, and we will always be sorry that we were not true to ourselves. My wife is always cautioning me about making promises and overcommitting myself, trying to make people happy in my enthusiasm—"Please come and visit us," and "I will be glad to preach for you"—later realizing I cannot possibly keep my promise.

Any repressed guilt, therefore, often evokes an attitude that is contrary to our truest feelings. It is far better to get in touch with our honest feelings. I know what it is to sit down to eat and make myself like a particular food, especially if I am with a friend who insists that I try it. If I don't like something, I tend to eat it first, trying hard to like it. Then I am upset with myself for filling up on something I did not enjoy. We can do this with people, trying so hard to fit in, please everybody, and like everybody.

The truth is, we don't have to like everybody. The American comedian Will Rogers used to say there are only two kinds of people: those you like and those you don't know. But there is, in fact, a third category—those you don't like! We don't have to like everybody. We are required to show love, forgiveness, and kindness to everybody, but you don't have to like everybody. And when we don't like someone but repress it because we feel terrible for not liking them, we end up so often with egg on our faces.

One of the hardest things in the world for us to do is to get in touch with our feelings. What I mean is how we really feel. I think that good psychological health might be measured by the time it takes between the moment when we repress what we feel and the moment when we consciously admit to what we feel. Good emotional health may be partly measured by closing the time gap between repression and honest admission. Some take years before they admit to their true feelings. Some take months; some, weeks; some, hours; some, minutes; and some, seconds. If we can close the time gap to seconds, we are getting in touch with how we really feel at the moment about this or that.

Take, for example, when you attend a church service or hear someone sing or preach. Your friends around you are enjoying it, but it is not your kind of music, singing, or preaching. Your friends are going on about what a wonderful singer or preacher this person is or how great the worship is. So you chime in, "Yes, this is wonderful," and you tell yourself this for a good while. But then one day, somehow, you are able to see how you really feel—and probably truly felt—about this or that. You admit to yourself that you did not really enjoy what everybody else enjoyed. I am saying that it is far better for us to be totally honest with ourselves and not repress, rather than saying what gains the instant approval of those around us.

Repression is almost never good. If you push what you feel down into your subconscious it will often come out of your mouth eventually in an embarrassing way. If you push your feelings down into the cellar, they come out through the attic in high blood pressure, anger, anxiety, and depression, just to name a few possibilities. But repressing your feelings is so easy to do and often very hard not to do. It frequently comes from letting pseudoguilt govern your thoughts.

My grandmother used to make me feel guilty as I grew up by saying, "You won't always have Grandma; you had better appreciate me while you have me." She would say this when I was impudent or disobedient. I can recall hearing this when I was only six years old. I must admit, it worked. I began to listen to her and obey! I felt guilty for a long time that she was not my favorite relative. I resented this for years and truly felt guilty that I did not appreciate her as I should have. Indeed, after she died some thirty-five years later at the age of ninety-two, I realized I did not appreciate her as I should have. So she was right. But it was pseudoguilt she was putting on me. I think, however, I would have loved and appreciated her more had she not given me the guilt trip.

When I was fifteen, during the time my mother was pregnant with my little sister, I got into an argument with her. I now have no idea what it was about. I only remember that my mother cried a lot. It was put to me that if she miscarried my little sister, it would have been my fault. But that is not all; it was put to me a couple of years later that her heart condition, which brought on her death at the age of forty-three, may have been caused by me. This was very hard for me to take. I learned years later that her heart condition stemmed from rheumatic fever that she had when she was only nine years old and that I had nothing to do with her death.

An Overly Scrupulous Conscience

For some reason I have always had what could be called an overly scrupulous conscience. An overly scrupulous conscience involves trying to come up to an excessively high standard and letting almost anything under the sun make you feel unworthy, inferior, and guilty. I was not taught the doctrine of "once saved, always saved." I was taught that you risked losing your salvation by going to a cinema, wearing jewelry, buying ice cream on Sunday, reading a Sunday newspaper, losing your temper, playing basketball on Sunday, playing cards at any time, or not keeping all of the Ten Commandments. I grew up seldom knowing for sure if I was saved. I think my overly scrupulous conscience comes from the way I was taught at church and at home and the way my parents administered punishment.

I remember trying to play my dad's saxophone (they had a little band in the church) in the middle of the service at an inappropriate time. My dad abruptly took me downstairs and spanked me. I am told that everybody in the church auditorium heard me screaming.

This was just one way my dad felt led to discipline me. He would sometimes take me into the bedroom, take off his belt, then kneel and pray with me for divine guidance as to how many times he should strike me. I would cry as he would say, "Yes, Lord, three times." "Oh, no, Daddy. Please, please give me another chance."

My parents meant well. I loved my parents and would actually regard my dad as being the best man I ever knew. My dad did his best with me. His own father was a terror! Dad told me that he had vowed not to punish me as his own father punished him. I am sure that my dad was mild in his punishing me in comparison with his father. I take the view, however, that the way my parents disciplined me, combined with my church's teaching, had something to do with my having an overly scrupulous conscience. An overly scrupulous conscience is usually driven by pseudoguilt and fear.

As far back as I can remember I have had an obsessive preoccupation with time. When I first started driving our car at the age of sixteen I always had to be home by 11:00 p.m. I came in at 11:03 one night. There was my dad, standing at the door, pointing to his watch. I have an inordinate fear of wasting time, being late, being early, stopping at a café on a highway (seeing other cars getting down the road, which I should be doing), not getting enough done every day, not praying or reading my Bible enough, not getting enough done on a plane when flying, or watching TV I did not benefit from. I suppose this neurosis has its good points. I broke all academic records at my old seminary. I always got deacons' meetings over in less than two hours, and I am usually able to quit preaching on time. But the hypocrisy in all this is the lack of time I gave to my precious children as they were growing up, and I cannot get those years back.

When we grow up and see unfairness in our parents, we often vow, "If I am ever a parent, I will not repeat what my parents did to me." But we do. I did. I have no doubt whatsoever that I have been unnecessarily hard on our two children because of the way I was brought up.

As for an overly scrupulous conscience and pseudoguilt, a classic case that combines the two comes out of the Old Testament. It is what cost Uriah his life. He was summoned home by King David and told to have a quiet weekend with his wife, Bathsheba. Uriah did not know, of course, that he was being brought home to cover up David's sin of adultery with Bathsheba. But Uriah could not bring himself to go home to Bathsheba. Uriah's reason for refusing to sleep with his wife was he could not leave his fellow soldiers on the battlefield: "How could I go to my house to eat and drink and lie with my wife? As surely as you live, I will not do such a thing!" (2 Sam. 11:11). He would feel too guilty to do this. It was not true guilt but false. Pseudoguilt cost him his life!

HEART-WRENCHING EXAMPLES OF FALSE GUILT

I listed some illustrations of pseudoguilt above—all of them fairly trite examples. But there are far, far more serious examples of pseudoguilt. Some of these may exemplify what you have had to think through. Consider these scenarios:

- A man backs out of his garage, does not see his two-year-old son in the driveway, and runs over the child, who dies within minutes. This father will blame himself forever, but he did not mean to do what he did. It was not a sin, but pseudoguilt.

- A lady puts on the brakes of her car too late, then skids into the other lane and has a head-on collision. Four people in the other car die from the accident. She will be found guilty of careless driving in court, but she did not mean to hurt anybody, neither did she sin against God. It is pseudoguilt that will bother her from then on.

- A young man is ordered to shoot and kill in war; he cannot get over the guilt of taking other people's lives. This is pseudoguilt.

- A young lady is raped shortly after getting off the bus at night; she blames herself that she was not more watchful. This is another case of pseudoguilt.

- A nurse was late in arriving at a home where she was to give the patient an injection that might have saved the patient's life; the patient died moments before the nurse arrived. The nurse was ridden with guilt for years. But it was pseudoguilt.

- A father who did not bond adequately with his son and a domineering mother who gave the child "smother love" now blame themselves that their son is gay in his lifestyle. Whatever the failures of the parents— and who has not failed?—God does not hold them responsible for the way the son turned out; they suffer from pseudoguilt.

- A minister is awakened in the middle of the night by a threat on the other end of the line, "I am going to kill myself if you don't come and help me." The pastor, who dismisses the call as an idle threat, is ridden with guilt when he discovers the next day that the man on the phone committed suicide shortly afterward. The pastor suffers pseudoguilt from this.

A list like this could be endless. The point is, none of the examples above could be regarded as offenses toward God. No sin was involved, although these people understandably experienced tremendous guilt. The truth is, these are all examples of false guilt, however real and horrible it felt.

For this reason, pseudoguilt can sometimes be harder to cope with and deal with than true guilt. My heart aches for all of the above. I have not personally had to experience anything in my own life like the accounts I just described. I do know what it is to try to help people pastorally who have had these episodes in their lives. This is not the time to deal with the hard question, "Why does God allow things like this to happen?" I only know that He does allow bad things to happen—to "bad" people and "good" people (although none are truly *good* in God's sight; see Romans 3:12). "Time and chance happen to them all" (Eccles. 9:11).

WHEN GOD FORGIVES BUT YOU CAN'T FORGIVE YOURSELF

When you know God forgives you but you can't forgive yourself, you are dealing—at first—with false guilt. It is not right that you do not forgive yourself; it is wrong. But it becomes sinful if you don't eventually accept both God's forgiveness *and* your own forgiveness. I will explain this further later. In the meantime, you should know what I will be stressing throughout this book: as God totally forgives you for your sinful past—it will not be held against you—so also you should totally forgive yourself and not allow your past to haunt you. It is highly displeasing to God for you not to forgive yourself, and it is highly pleasing to Satan when you do not forgive yourself. Do you want to please the devil? I don't think so!

Here are some examples of people who have been forgiven but cannot forgive themselves. I have added brief comments as to the way forward for each of these:

- A man who was convicted of driving under the influence of alcohol—and charged with manslaughter for the deaths of people in a car accident—has since come to Christ and has asked God to forgive him. He believes God has forgiven him all his sins, including killing innocent people. But he cannot forgive himself or let himself off the hook. This man needs to forgive himself; otherwise he will fall into unbelief and have to answer to God for not truly accepting his own forgiveness. If he does not forgive himself, he will be accountable for not accepting the forgiveness God offers him. Pseudoguilt becomes true guilt if not dealt with.

- A man was unfaithful to his wife. She divorced him. He has since been forgiven by God, but he cannot forgive himself for what he did to his wife. But he must forgive himself; otherwise he will lapse into self-pity, which is a sin.

- An alcoholic, converted as an older man, can barely remember his children as they grew up, and he feels the guilt of the wasted years. But he needs to move on and enjoy God's forgiveness; otherwise the devil wins a victory, which does not need to happen.

- A Christian lady who had kept herself pure for years and years slept with a man in a weak moment—once. But she got pregnant and became a single parent. She knows God forgave her, but she cannot forgive herself for her mistake or for the fact that her son knows no male authority figure in his life. Hard as this is for her, she must let the past be past—and trust utterly in Romans 8:28, that all things work together for good to them who love God and are called according to His purpose.

- A young lady had an abortion. She later asks God's forgiveness and wishes she had kept the child. This too will work together for good if she will forgive herself and get her joy from God's approval of her through the blood of Jesus.

- A busy career woman who is married with no children had an affair and an abortion and does not tell her husband, and then she feels ashamed. She confesses it to God but cannot forgive herself. This too is another hard case, but, though this is a dark sin indeed, God is good and merciful and will work this for good—if she will trust Him and not her own feelings.

- A married man who carried on a secret gay lifestyle gave his wife AIDS. He believes God has forgiven him, but he cannot forgive himself. Romans 8:28 is true for this and all cases—no matter how deep the sin.

- A gay man becomes a Christian, repents of his homosexual activity, and changes his ways, but he remains gay in his orientation and feels guilty that he still fights the same old temptation. This is pseudoguilt he is experiencing—unless he returns to his old lifestyle. He needs to accept himself and not condemn himself for his orientation.

- A murderer and bank robber is converted in prison and accepts God's total forgiveness, but he is so far unable to forgive himself for the people he murdered and the damage done to so many. A person like this feels guilty for not having guilt. He feels that the guilty feeling is part of his just punishment. But this becomes self-righteousness—a sin before God. It would seem too good to be true for him to be set free and totally forgive himself. But that is precisely what God wants him to do.

- A man who was abused as a child abused his own children as they grew up. He has been converted but feels an incalculable guilt for the way he messed up his kids' minds—and cannot get over it. This is another difficult case. He must release his children to God and trust that they will find their joy in Christ. In the meantime, this man must accept God's forgiveness and not look back into the past but know that this too will work for good if he loves God.

I sympathize with every example I have shared with you. It is certainly not necessarily easy to forgive yourself of a sinful past even though you know that God has forgiven you. But it is something you should do, something God wants *you* to do (whatever is in your own past), and something that will bring you joy unspeakable. I promise it. You may then struggle with guilt over being so full of joy! You might even think to yourself, "I don't deserve to have this joy. I should be punished." But that is precisely what the devil will encourage you to believe.

The truth is, we are all sinners. As the late Dr. Peter Eldersveld, the radio preacher of the *Back to God Hour,* put it: "I am a sinner—great as any, worse than many." Yes, that's me. But I am also a forgiven man. I refuse to dignify the devil, Christ's archenemy, by not accepting God's total forgiveness and by not totally forgiving myself. I refuse to let any human being give me a guilt trip for my failures. I want to understand where such people are coming from and not point the finger at them. But I will not let myself, another person, or Satan himself keep me from honoring the blood Jesus shed on the cross for my sins.

Forgiving yourself is not repression. It is not denial of your sinful past. It is not refusing to look at the bad things you have done. In *Total Forgiveness* I point out that we do not deny what people have done to us in order to forgive them. We don't shut our eyes to it. It is with eyes wide open to what they have done that we *totally* forgive them! So too with ourselves.

Feeling guilty after knowing God forgives you, then, is pseudo-guilt. That feeling of guilt does not come from God. But when you try to get to the bottom of it, you will realize that dwelling on false guilt is exploring a bottomless pit that will lead you to despair. It will become sinful if not dealt with. Confess your failure to forgive yourself to God! Admit *not forgiving yourself as a sin* that needs to be cleansed by the blood of Christ as much as any other sin. Then refuse to dwell on it—ever again.

Learning to be honest with your true feelings, and not repressing them, will help you to be able to recognize and identify false guilt in yourself. But the best way you overcome it is not through endless psychotherapy but, as I will emphasize later, through esteeming the pleasure of God more than pleasing people and our-selves. In a word, once we see that our pain is actually from false guilt, we should refuse to let it dominate us! But admittedly that is easier said than done, and this book is written to help you in this area. Sometimes the very knowledge of what pseudoguilt *is* causes a lot of the pain to diminish. I know that I myself have been greatly helped merely by realizing that we all have pseudoguilt, but its origin is not God! God does not want me to listen to what is not from Him. Satan does!

What has helped me to no end is realizing that giving in to false guilt is showing insufficient esteem for the honor that would come from God. That is precisely what I don't want to miss—the praise He wants to bestow. I will say it again: pseudoguilt is never from God. When I give it my attention and let it control me, I am showing more respect for pseudoguilt than I do for the glory that God wants to give. I do not want to forfeit what He Himself would bestow on me. I have sought to be governed by John 5:44: "How can you believe if you accept praise from one another, yet make no effort to obtain the praise that comes from the only God?" Therefore paying homage to pseudoguilt is to dignify the flesh—and esteem guilt that God did not put there. I do not want to give the flesh such dignity, much less the devil, who will exploit pseudoguilt whenever he can.

False guilt should be treated as temptation, recognized for what it is, then refused and resisted. Refuse to think about it. It is not a sin to have pseudoguilt; it is a sin to let it dominate you. As the old saying goes, "You can't keep the birds from flying over your head, but you can keep them from nesting in your hair!" It is a sin not to reject pseudoguilt once you realize what it is, and then to let it cast you down.

There is a difference between temptation and sin; it is not a sin to be tempted (James 1:13–15). Jesus was tempted (Heb. 4:15). It is a sin when you give in to temptation, which Jesus never did (1 Pet. 2:22). Some people feel guilty merely because they are tempted. This too is pseudoguilt. The devil will exploit this as well. Who among us can help it if we are tempted? God does not want you to feel guilty because you are tempted. If, however, you do succumb to temptation and go against God's revealed will, then sin has been committed and true guilt now exists.

False guilt leads to anxiety, depression, arthritis, irritability, and ill health of all sorts. I am so glad that we are invited to cast all our anxiety on the Lord—He cares for us (1 Pet. 5:7). Giving Him our anxiety enables us to participate in Jesus's own experience, for He said, "My yoke is easy and my burden is light" (Matt. 11:30). The person who can say that feels no guilt—not the slightest bit.

Jesus never felt guilty. He never felt guilt of any kind, except when He was bearing *our* sins on the cross. But until that moment Jesus never felt guilty—ever. He wants that total freedom from guilt for you and me.

CHAPTER 3

TRUE GUILT

There is no one righteous, not even one; there is no one who understands, no one who seeks God. All have turned away, they have together become worthless; there is no one who does good, not even one... so that every mouth may be silenced and the whole world held accountable [guilty (KJV)] to God.... Through the law we become conscious of sin.... For all have sinned and fall short of the glory of God.

—ROMANS 3:10–23

If we claim to be without sin, we deceive ourselves and the truth is not in us. If we confess our sins, he is faithful and just and will forgive us our sins and purify us from all unrighteousness.

—1 JOHN 1:8–9

I have come to the conclusion that none of us in our generation feels as guilty about sin as we should or as our forefathers did. I think this basically is the problem of living in a psychologically oriented age.

—FRANCIS SCHAEFFER[1]

It is difficult to say which is a more apt description of our age: the "me" generation that describes our self-centeredness, or the "blame" generation that shrinks from personal responsibility and attaches fault to anything and anyone but ourselves. The funny thing is, even a good case of *false* guilt is alien to some people! We are living in a day in which people are sometimes encouraged to feel no guilt about anything.

The psychologist Lawrence Kohlberg (1927–1987) theorized that people progress in their moral reasoning through a series of stages. The first level of moral thinking, generally found at the elementary school level, is that people behave according to socially acceptable norms because they are told to do so by some authority figure (e.g., parent or teacher). This obedience is compelled by the threat or application of punishment and is characterized by an attitude that seeks to do what will gain the approval of others. The second stage is characterized by a view that right behavior means acting in one's own best interests. This is sometimes called conventional morality. The third level, which Kohlberg felt was *not reached by the majority of adults,* is based on respect for universal principles and the demands of individual conscience. Sadly, some people never attain to the understanding that their conduct has greater consequences outside themselves.[2]

The result is that some people—apart from any degree of Christian influence—never develop a good conscience. As a consequence of this, there will be no need for some to forgive themselves; they never felt any sense of shame in the first place! It shows how far we have drifted in our society from a respectable standard of ethics and morality and how far we are indeed from any sense of guilt toward our Creator and biblical morality. However, for those of us seeking to forgive ourselves, we need to recognize *true* guilt and how to deal with it.

True guilt is culpability before God. God holds us responsible for our *sins*. He does not judge us for our temptations or weaknesses. He does not judge us for having pseudoguilt. We all experience this. But false guilt is a weakness that must be resisted and, as I said earlier, not allowed to lead to sin. It is not a sin to have a weakness, and not every weakness in us necessarily leads to sin. Furthermore, not all temptations lead to sin, and, as I said earlier, it is not a sin to be tempted. There is a difference between temptation and sin. After all, Jesus was tempted and did not sin (Heb. 4:15). We are only responsible to God for our *sins*.

For this reason, however, like it or not, we are all guilty before Him since "all have sinned and fall short" of His glory (Rom. 3:23). The context of Romans 3:23, apart from showing the universality of sin, should also help us not to be surprised at our many imperfections. But at the same time God requires that we answer to Him for all our ungodly thoughts, attitudes, words, and actions. It is unlikely that we will live through an entire day without having to draw upon the grace offered in 1 John 1:9: "If we confess our sins, he is faithful and just and will forgive us our sins and purify us from all unrighteousness." This is because the "best" of God's people are imperfect in this life.

We all sin every day, but I do not refer here to overt, scandalous sins, for sins like these are resistible. A Christian never needs to commit awful sins like these. After all, some sins *are* worse than others. But the truth is, we *do* sin in His sight through pride, fear, and unbelief day after day. We are all found wanting, and we should learn that we all owe an incalculable debt to our Creator for our sins. Not only that; this guilt is *there* whether we feel it or not.

Here is the irony all too often: the guilt we should feel, we don't; the guilt we shouldn't feel, we do. The guilt therefore we often feel is pseudoguilt.

You will recall that pseudoguilt is a false sense of shame but very real to us indeed. True guilt, however, may not seem "real" to us—that is, we can be utterly unaware of it. God charges us as being culpable, which means that we deserve blame for offending Him. But strange as it may seem, we often feel *absolutely nothing* for what we have done that is truly wrong in His eyes.

To put it another way, *deserving* blame and *feeling* that we are to be blamed is not the same thing. God is the One who delivers the verdict. True guilt therefore exists, whether we agree with His high standard and opinion or not. This guilt exists whether we are conscious of sin or not. True guilt thus refers to the *fact* of our offense toward God and that we deserve the blame for our sin. Therefore, unlike pseudoguilt, which we all feel, true guilt may not be felt at all.

On the other hand, the Bible talks about a conscience "seared as with a hot iron" (1 Tim. 4:2). First Timothy 4:1–2 refers to the influence of the demonic upon teachers who are "hypocritical liars." Such people may feel no guilt of any kind—whether pseudo-guilt or true guilt. A seared conscience also explains the conduct of some people who can commit the most heinous crimes without any regret. It would seem that such people either have managed to repress at the most extreme level so that they feel nothing for wrongdoing, or they are the victim of Satan. They never experience true guilt and feel little, if any, pseudoguilt. Apart from God's overruling graciousness, such individuals will not change. In any case, they will not likely feel the need to read this book.

There are basically two ways by which we become conscious of guilt:

1. Our conscience
2. The Holy Spirit showing us our sin and leading us to the remedy

The conscience is an innate sense of right and wrong—we are all born with it, which leaves us without excuse (Rom. 1:20). But the conscience does not show the remedy. Although it is capable of making us feel ashamed, it is not capable of setting us free. It is the conscience that is also the vehicle of pseudoguilt. It is therefore an unreliable instrument when it comes to moving us effectually toward true freedom. It is only the Holy Spirit that can both show us our sin and lead to our consciences being cleansed by the blood of Christ (Heb. 9:14). The Holy Spirit will never lead us to pseudoguilt, which the conscience can sometimes do; the Holy Spirit shows us true guilt before God but also the way that guilt is dealt with, namely, by trusting Jesus's death on the cross, whose blood atoned for all our sins.

To summarize what I have said in this chapter so far, the whole world is declared guilty before God since "all have sinned" (Rom. 3:23), but no one necessarily feels shame for their sin. Whereas offending the Most Holy God results in the kind of guilt that ought to grip us, shake us rigid, and alarm us to our fingertips, we will never be truly convicted of sin unless the Holy Spirit mercifully reveals it.

Part of our natural depravity is blindness and stubbornness. You may ask, "Why is it that the very act of sin does not make us instantly sense our guilt and debt to God?" It is because this sense of sin never takes place apart from the Holy Spirit showing it to us. As we will see in more detail in chapter 7, David committed murder and adultery but was not apparently convicted or bothered by it until the prophet Nathan came to him.

Why does pseudoguilt grip us when we have done nothing truly wrong, but sin that incurs true guilt may make no impact on us whatsoever? It is because we are miserable sinners. That's why we often feel *nothing* when we offend God. Surely, we may think, the most obvious cause of guilt and anxiety—our sin against God—is what should send us on a heavy, conscious guilt trip. But it seldom does. We tend to be far more occupied with pseudoguilt than we are with what offends our heavenly Father.

For example, we are often more concerned about being late for an appointment, innocently upsetting someone, or performing well than we are about our sin. We can stay awake thinking we did not get enough done that day but sleep like a baby when we have not cared for the poor or witnessed to lost people around us. We are far more bothered over what people say about us than what dishonors God's Son. We are more consumed with anger when we are lied about than with feelings of remorse when we grieve the Holy Spirit by gossip.

It is therefore because of a blind spot in us that we don't tend to feel deeply about what ought to make us embarrassed before God and the angels. The apostle Paul said that it is the "god of this world" (Satan) who blinds us to our sin and responsibility and leads us away from God's will (2 Cor. 4:4, KJV). This is what keeps people from becoming converted. But Satan continues to do all he can to blind us, which apparently happened to David after his sin.

How easily, then, do we dismiss the beggar with his hand out, the drunkard in the gutter, or the poor man who has no job and go on our way with almost no pang of conscience? We flirt with the opposite sex, speak unkindly about an enemy, manifest jealousy over another's success, and gloat when a rival is brought down. None of these things tend to drive us to our knees in contrition. But let someone criticize us, and we are devastated; brag on us, and we are elated; accuse us, and we are indignant and defensive; flatter us, and we enjoy it.

True guilt is the last thing we tend to feel very deeply about. Pseudoguilt commands our attention in seconds. It is part of the human, sinful condition that will war against us until we die. In this life we live in jars of clay, and the very best of God's servants are imperfect (2 Cor. 4:7). In the words of a hymn, "Prone to wander, Lord, I feel it, prone to leave the God I love," the author expressed what every conscientious Christian should feel.[3] But if the Holy Spirit does not give us a sense of sin, we remain unbothered by things that should bring us to tears.

Isaiah apparently had a respectable prophetic ministry without any great sense of sin. But when he saw the glory of the Lord, he cried out, "Woe to me!...I am ruined! For I am a man of unclean lips, and I live among a people of unclean lips, and my eyes have seen the King, the LORD Almighty" (Isa. 6:5). That is what the Holy Spirit did. Moreover, Isaiah was not left in that state. God never leaves us like that; Isaiah was cleansed and assured that his "guilt [was] taken away and [his] sin atoned for" (Isa. 6:7). It is not that Isaiah had been living in any scandalous sin prior to this moment; he no doubt was an upright, clean servant of God. But the Holy Spirit convicted him of sin he could not otherwise have been aware of.

When therefore I refer to a *sense of sin*, I am certainly not referring to engaging in any sinful act. Some sincere Christians have not been taught along these lines and can only imagine a sense of sin coming from having committed some awful, overt evil act. The funny thing is, as we have seen, some people can commit overt acts of blatant wrongdoing and feel nothing! Others sense a conviction of sin by merely being in the presence of God. For the presence of God can make us see things about ourselves that we are unable to see were it not for the Holy Spirit showing us our wrong. Without the Spirit of God convicting us, we do things that are sinful and never feel the slightest sense of wrong—like the unkind retort, holding a grudge, boasting of yourself to clear your name, running ahead of God, and saying something about another that makes them look bad.

A sense of sin, then, is having a conscience that is sensitive to the Holy Spirit who reveals sin to us. This is partly why I wrote *The Sensitivity of the Spirit*. The Holy Spirit, when we develop a mature sensitivity to Him and His ways, will overrule our natural proneness to repress what is true. You will recall that repression is a defense mechanism in us that will deny what is true. It is the gracious Holy Spirit who will not let us sweep the dirt under the carpet. The Holy Spirit convicts us of fear, pride, making ungracious comments, thoughts that are counterproductive, neglecting the needs of others, not to mention anything that brings disgrace upon God's name. It is therefore a part of our human nature to repress a sense of sin.

It is a most wonderful blessing to be convicted of sin. It is a sign you are loved. "We love because he first loved us" (1 John 4:19). When God reveals to you and me our sin, we should not resent it or become defensive but fall on our knees and thank Him! We should equally feel that way when we are judged for our sin—as being found out. It is a sign that we are loved and that God isn't finished with us when we are judged; it is true repentance God is after—not making us feel guilty.

One thing that will help us see our sin is to realize how much God hates sin and how dangerous it is to play fast and loose with sin. Whereas we may be tempted to edge as close to the world, the flesh, and the devil as we can without crossing over a line, true conviction of sin will make us live as far from that line as we can. Sin is not only what led Jesus to die on a cross; it is what will destroy us if not seen, repented of, and turned away from.

Since I began writing this very chapter the news on all the television channels is about another Christian leader who has been found in immorality. On the very day I appeared on Dr. James Dobson's radio broadcast, which reaches the entire world, as we warned of impending judgment from God because of a nation abandoning biblical principles of righteousness and morality, the secular news was exploiting the news of a fallen church leader to the hilt. Some high-profile Christians—leaders, big givers, high-powered businesspeople, deacons, elders, TV personalities, preachers—seem to think that their importance and the good they do for the church will offset their secret sins and that they therefore will be protected from judgment. Wrong. It grieves God to do it, but He brings judgment upon the very "best" of His servants—as in the case of King David, a man after His own heart. The news of a high-profile church leader getting "caught" and openly ridiculed by the worldly media ought to warn you and me not to see how close we can edge to the world but how far away we can stay from it. God won't bend the rules for any of us.

Apart from pointing to their ultimate fulfillment in Jesus Christ, one of the reasons for the sacrificial system in ancient Israel, with all its ritual and carefully thought-out details, was to show the seriousness of sin. The sacrifices were "an annual reminder of sins" (Heb. 10:3). God brought in the Law and the sacrifices of animals to atone for sin because of the sins of the people (Gal. 3:19). He hated their sin but loved *them*. He provided a way whereby sin could be atoned for—through the substitution of an animal. But when the people persisted in their sins even after the sacrificial system was put in place, God still judged His people. This is because He intends that those who trust in the sacrifice He provides must also obey Him and show gratitude for their being forgiven.

THE TEN COMMANDMENTS

Sin, then, is an offense toward God. The Ten Commandments contain laws that pertain to sin directly against God Himself by our not worshiping and serving Him alone. The command "You shall have no other gods before me" (Exod. 20:3) points to how you and I are to relate to God Himself. He is a jealous God. When anything competes with Him, He sees this as sin. The command about having an idol is also showing what offends God. So too the misuse of His name is sin in His eyes (vv. 4–7).

Sin is so horrible in God's sight that the very first sermon of the New Testament was that of John the Baptist warning us to "flee from the coming wrath" of God (Matt. 3:7). The coming wrath ultimately referred to hell—the everlasting lot of those whose sins are not washed by the blood of Christ. If God thought that hell was right to create—after all, it was His idea, not that of any human being—sin must be far, far more horrendous in His eyes than you and I can fathom.

During the course of writing this chapter, I took some preaching engagements in New England. I took advantage of being near Enfield, Connecticut. Louise and I rented a car, drove to Enfield, and stood on the spot where Jonathan Edwards preached his famous sermon "Sinners in the Hands of an Angry God" in July 1741. Taking his text from Deuteronomy 32:35, "Their foot shall slide in due time" (KJV), Edwards graphically demonstrated to his hearers how blessed they were not to be in hell as he preached, that they could slide right into hell at any moment, and that the very mercy of God had prevented them from being in hell. The Spirit of God fell on the people. A sense of sin gripped them. They began to groan audibly as he preached. Such a fear of God came upon them that men were seen holding to church pews to keep from sliding into hell. Men outside were holding to tree trunks to keep from slipping into hell. This event came at the height of the Great Awakening. If you ask why Louise and I prayed at this spot, it was because I wanted to thank God for the sermon that has influenced my life and ministry so strongly—and also to ask God to "do it again."

What is missing in the church more than anything in the world at the present time is the fear of God and a sense of sin.

The Holy Spirit brings to light how much God hates sin and how grieved He is with us when we indulge in it. The reason for the repeated references to the fear of God, particularly in Luke and Acts, is to show how men and women truly feel once the Spirit of God has come down in power. (See Luke 5:26; 7:16; 8:37; 12:5; Acts 2:43; 5:5, 11; 19:17.) This is the way many people felt during much of the time of the Great Awakening in the eighteenth century. I say it again: it is what is almost entirely absent today. What is needed more than anything in the world is a restoration of the fear of God in the land, especially among Christians. When true revival comes to the church, and I for one believe it is on the way, people will feel much the same way as Isaiah did, as we saw above.

True guilt also has its origin in sinning against people. The Ten Commandments do not only mention sins that offend God's honor and name. He makes us equally answerable to sins against people—murder, adultery, stealing, and lying (Exod. 20:13–16). When I sin against another person, it is also sin against God. Murder is sin against the person but equally sin against God, because one has broken His Law that forbids murder. Committing adultery is sin against the person one slept with, but it is equally sin against God. When I do not feed the hungry or visit the person in prison, I sin against the Lord Jesus. The problem is, when I neglect people like this, I too often don't feel a thing. Sorry, but that is the way we all are. We will find out at the final judgment that, though we did not feel anything at the time—protesting to the Lord Jesus, "When did we see you hungry or thirsty...or needing clothes or sick or in prison, and did not help you?" (Matt. 25:44)—we will discover that we sinned against Christ Himself.

The key to understanding and experiencing true guilt is a good relationship with God. There is no substitute for this. All have sinned and fall short of the glory of God, but not all feel bad that they sin and fall short of the glory of God. It is only when a relationship with the God of the Bible is our highest priority that we feel guilty as we should when we sin against God.

Had Joseph succumbed to the temptation of sleeping with Potiphar's wife, he would have sinned against her, her husband, and himself. But what concerned Joseph—his ultimate reason for refusing to sleep with her—was that doing so would be a wicked "sin against God" (Gen. 39:9). His stalwart character in the face of sexual temptation was manifest because, despite all his faults, he had a good relationship with God. That is what mattered ultimately to him and what preserved him. Most people I know avoid sexual sin merely because they fear they will get caught if they give in. Joseph had an opportunity—as good as it probably gets—to sin and get away with it. Potiphar's wife would not tell her husband, and nobody back in Canaan (Joseph's family) would hear about it. But Joseph's relationship with God held him true.

This was also the case when David committed adultery with Bathsheba, to which we will return below. He sinned against her, her husband, and himself. But what grieved him most—eventually—was what the sin had done to his relationship with God: "Against you, you only, have I sinned and done what is evil in your sight" (Ps. 51:4). And yet, as I just said, this conviction of sin did not emerge in David's heart until he was confronted by the prophet Nathan (2 Sam. 12). This is amazing! He sinned as grievously as anybody described in the Old Testament, having committed adultery and murder, but did not apparently feel bad about it until Nathan approached him some two years later. The backslider is indeed "filled with his own ways" (Prov. 14:14, KJV). It is like straining out a gnat but swallowing a camel (Matt. 23:24)! Truly, the heart is deceitful above all things and desperately—incurably—wicked (Jer. 17:9).

JESUS'S INTERPRETATION OF THE TEN
COMMANDMENTS: THE SERMON ON THE MOUNT

I need to refer again to "a sense of sin"—that is, feeling conviction of sin and being acutely aware of what grieves the Holy Spirit. This sense of sin is partly what Jesus was aiming at in the Sermon on the Mount. He no doubt shocked His hearers when He said that we cannot inherit the kingdom of heaven unless our righteousness "surpasses" that of the Pharisees (Matt. 5:20).

It surely goes without saying that overt sins like murder or adultery bring one under God's condemnation. This would be true with all the Ten Commandments that are unfolded and interpreted in the New Testament. Therefore I have chosen to deal not only with undeniable overt sins that bring one under true guilt but also sins that the Holy Spirit would bring to one's attention should a person develop a consciousness of what grieves the Spirit (Eph. 4:30). I say this because totally forgiving ourselves can only be achieved ultimately by an acute sense of sin, which must be repented of and abandoned if you want true freedom.

Based upon the teachings of Jesus, here are examples of true guilt:

- A man was promised a promotion in his company. Someone else got the job but achieved it by telling lies about the man who was promised it. Those in charge believed the lies. This man, a Christian, resented what had happened and vowed to get vengeance. He began defending himself and saying unkind things about the person who got the promotion. One sympathizes with this man's deep hurt, but sadly he sinned along the way. He may or may not have felt any guilt for his efforts to vindicate himself, but the truth is he has incurred true guilt and eventually has to answer for it. How do we know he sinned? Because of Jesus's interpretation of the sixth command: "You shall not murder" (Exod. 20:13). The anger the man felt violated Jesus's teachings even though he did not physically kill anybody. But according to Jesus, the man's anger, or hate, was sin (Matt. 5:21–26). Were the man to see the error of his ways, all he would need to do is acknowledge his sin to God, repent of it, and cease doing anything to vindicate himself. True guilt need not be harbored or carried for any length of time. It is not what God wants at all. True guilt is usually felt only for a moment or two, then confessed to God, who instantly forgives. God does not say, "You did not feel guilty long enough," or, "You don't seem sufficiently sorry." God is not like that. Once we see our sin, confess, and repent of it, as far as God is concerned, *it's over*. Nothing more is needed. One accepts God's forgiveness and forgives oneself. But in this particular case, the man continued to try to vindicate himself. Sadly, he felt no guilt whatsoever, as far as one could tell.

• An evangelist, too often away from home and unhappily married, gave his altar call, and a very attractive young lady came forward. This evangelist volunteered to give her a time of follow-up and counseling. The eventual result was that they had an affair. He divorced his wife and married this woman. According to the Law in Deuteronomy 24:1–5, one could divorce his wife for any reason under the sun. But according to Jesus, this evangelist and new wife are living in sin (Matt. 5:31–32). Neither person in this marriage apparently felt any guilt for what they did. This is often the case when one ought to feel true guilt but doesn't. The person feels nothing. But unless there is an unfeigned repentance, the approval of God will be withheld from this couple. Were they to acknowledge their sin and truly repent, God would forgive them and they should be able to forgive themselves. They don't need to go back to the past; they can have a future. Divorce as described in this case is truly sin, but God forgives sin. Sadly, this couple, as far as I can tell, felt no conviction of sin whatsoever. It is a case of true guilt; no awareness of sin seems evident. Sometimes people refuse to admit the grossest of sins but dig their heels in instead.

• A pastor's wife became attracted to the worship leader in their church. She began to let him know how she felt. The result was that he reciprocated and expressed his feelings for her. They never had any physical involvement with each other, however. It was all in conversations—whenever they could meet or talk on the phone. But in the meantime, neither was attracted to his or her own spouse. Their own marriages were "dead." What is more, neither felt the slightest guilt over what was going on; after all, they did not touch each other, much less sleep with each other. But according to Jesus they committed adultery in their hearts because of their lust. What is more, the pastor's wife, who initiated the "affair," actually *caused* the worship leader to lust after her. According to some evangelical Greek scholars, that is the real meaning of Matthew 5:28. Looking at one "lustfully" could be translated "causing to lust," which the woman did to the man in this case. This went on for a good while. Eventually they did sleep together. The result: two marriages and two ministries were destroyed. And as far as we know, there never was a feeling of guilt!

• A man with a prophetic gift (I will call him Prophet John) was criticized by another "prophet" (Prophet Bill). (I'm sure you have heard of "professional jealousy," but have you ever heard of "prophetic jealousy"? Well, it exists, too!) Prophet John, who was perhaps unfairly criticized, in order to vindicate himself brought God's name into the matter. That was his mistake. When Jesus said, "Do not swear at all" (Matt. 5:34), He was explaining the true meaning of the third commandment, "You shall not misuse the name of the LORD your God" (Exod. 20:7). When a person brings God's name in, in order to bolster their claim, they abuse God's holy name. Prophet John invoked the name of God, claiming to speak for God, and declared that God told him that Prophet Bill was in grievous error and would be severely judged for it. So it was prophet versus prophet. Prophet John should have overlooked what Prophet Bill had said about him, but he could not avoid taking it all personally. His emotions got in the way, and, worst of all, he brought the high name of God down to his pitifully silly level. Prophet John's calling down God's wrath on Prophet Bill immediately backfired. It made Prophet John look bad before everybody at the time. And the ultimate result was that it was Prophet John who was openly judged. Saddest yet, Prophet John felt no guilt in bringing God's name into this petty debate. People with lesser or no prophetic gifts do this, too. They say, "God told me this," and "God told me that." One should be very careful here. This is misusing God's name. People do it with doctrine, arguing over which church is true, which person is right, whether God is truly at work here or there, and if so-and-so has been led by the Holy Spirit. To make judgments like this may be innocent—until they bring in the lofty name of God. That is the sin. But people do it from every part of the church! And they should feel awful for it! It should bring us to feel true guilt, but sadly, it seldom does.

Only when a relationship with the God of the Bible means more to us than anything in the world will we be seriously bothered by *true* guilt. Pseudoguilt affects everybody without them doing anything truly wrong—saved or lost; Jew or Gentile; red, yellow, black, or white; male or female; young or old; Christian or non-Christian. For it does not take the Holy Spirit to give a person pseudoguilt. Indeed, the Holy Spirit does not ever produce pseudoguilt in us. He only convicts us of true guilt. Pseudoguilt gets our immediate attention without the help of the Holy Spirit.

It is only the Holy Spirit, then, who can give us a sense of shame or guilt when we have sinned against God. Part of our fleshly nature is to repress sin, whether voluntarily or involuntarily, and not to let it bother us. We excuse it, deny it, justify it, minimize it, and forget it. It is a solid relationship with God the Father, God the Son, and God the Holy Spirit that ensures we will not get away with sin against God.

Sometimes, however, it takes us years before we see our true guilt. This was my own case. At the beginning of this book I referred to my own sense of failure as a father. It started early. Before we came to England, when I was a student at Southern Baptist Theological Seminary in Louisville, Kentucky, I wanted to get my academic work behind me as soon as possible. I reasoned that if I would get this quickly behind me, then I would give the kids the time they needed. I did a three-year course in two years. I spent so little time with my two precious children. As I write these lines I am horrified at myself and have to resist the temptation to dwell on it and let it get me down.

But that is only the beginning. When we came to England and I had my first meeting with my supervisor at Oxford University, Dr. Barrie White, I only remember one thing he said to me: "Spend time with your children; you will never get these years back." That was a warning from the Lord. To be fair, we did have some memorable times, and I could perhaps say more, but it would be self-serving to do so. The truth is, I wanted to get my research at Oxford behind me as quickly as possible so I could return to the ministry and then, of course, I would have plenty of time for the children. I justified the endless hours at the Bodleian Library on the basis that the sooner I finished, the better.

But there is more. I accepted the call to be the minister of Westminster Chapel. Now I was in the ministry. Yes! But this time my problem was that I needed to preach the best sermons possible. I spent hours and hours preparing sermons—far more time than Dr. Martyn Lloyd-Jones did when he was there (he told me so). But I felt the need to do this. I reasoned that putting my preaching and church first was putting *God* first. Wrong. I now believe that I would have preached just as well had I put my family first—not sermon preparation. I could weep as I write if it were not for the fact I know God has forgiven me—and I have forgiven myself.

You will ask: "Was this *true* guilt—not spending time with your family—guilt before God?" Yes. I let God down by letting my family down. Children spell love t-i-m-e. I wish now I had spent more time with them and less time with church concerns. God would have been pleased, and I believe I would have preached as well if not better than I did. But it is too late now.

What do I do? I have asked for God's forgiveness—and received it. And then, which was harder, I forgave myself. I feel ashamed in letting myself off the hook like this, but this is what I am now required to do. Perhaps my example will help some younger preacher who reads these lines. And perhaps my example will also help *you* forgive yourself, too (for whatever failure you feel guilty about).

I have a feeling that some other parents have much the same problem—that perhaps you too have an equivalent problem. Maybe you have not spent adequate time with your own children. If so, you will know exactly what I am talking about. So if you are one of those busy people in the office and you come home tired and don't feel like spending time with the kids, or one of those who have big plans to get ahead, make money, get a promotion, or whatever, but realize in your heart that you are neglecting those children, just remember that there is forgiveness for all of us. Accept God's forgiveness. If it's not too late, change! If it seems too late, then forgive yourself.

So it is not pseudoguilt but true guilt I feel regarding my lack of time with my family, even if it took the years of accumulated neglect to set in and convict me. But I have forgiven myself—totally—and I lean hard on my verse in Romans 8:28 that says "all things" work together for good to them that love God and are called according to His purpose.

As for pseudoguilt, I could let that enter in if I ponder long about my failure. But one thing I know: I am forgiven. Therefore any "guilty feeling" that remains would not be from God. I therefore refuse to let any sense of shame that is not from the Holy Spirit govern me. Away with it—forever!

The purpose of this book could be summarized right here. If you and I can make the distinction in our minds between true guilt, and deal with it, and pseudoguilt, and not be governed by it, we are on our way to inner peace and freedom.

RESTITUTION

There is, however, one thing that one must do in connection with true guilt, should it apply, and that is making restitution. If the Law was a "shadow" of things to come (Heb. 10:1), we are obliged to learn from it whenever we can. Restitution is restoring a thing to the proper owner. It can also mean reparation for injury, which is like making amends or giving compensation. Here are examples of it in the Law:

> A thief must certainly make restitution, but if he has nothing, he must be sold to pay for his theft. . . . If a man grazes his livestock in a field or vineyard and lets them stray and they graze in another man's field, he must make restitution from the best of his own field or vineyard. If a fire breaks out and spreads into thornbushes so that it burns shocks of grain or standing grain or the whole field, the one who started the fire must make restitution. If a man gives his neighbor silver or goods for safekeeping and they are stolen from the neighbor's house, the thief, if he is caught, must pay back double.
>
> —Exodus 22:3–7

> If anyone sins and is unfaithful to the LORD by deceiving his neighbor about something entrusted to him or left in his care or stolen, or if he cheats him, or if he finds lost property

and lies about it, or if he swears falsely, or if he commits any such sin that people may do—when he thus sins and becomes guilty, he must return what he has stolen or taken by extortion, or what was entrusted to him, or the lost property he found, or whatever it was he swore falsely about. He must make restitution in full, add a fifth of the value to it and give it all to the owner on the day he presents his guilt offering. And as a penalty he must bring to the priest, that is, to the LORD, his guilt offering, a ram from the flock, one without defect and of the proper value. In this way the priest will make atonement for him before the LORD, and he will be forgiven for any of these things he did that made him guilty.

—LEVITICUS 6:2–7

Restitution was part of the civil law in ancient Israel and showed how the ancient people of God were to govern themselves and get along with each other. This should be applied to the Christian life *not* as a precondition to one's salvation but rather a formula for:

1. Maintaining peace in the fellowship of the church
2. Maintaining one's personal fellowship with God

In other words, restitution applies to those already *in* the family of God. It is not a requirement for becoming a Christian; otherwise our salvation would be based on good works, which it isn't (Eph. 2:8–9). Not all believers will find a need for restitution. But some will, and those who do must act accordingly if they:

- Want to have abiding fellowship with the Father
- Enjoy harmony with fellow Christians
- Forgive themselves

This means doing what you have to do in order to satisfy an offended party.

You may not always be able to make another person happy. But if you know that someone has something against you, and you know in your heart that you really did something wrong, you are required to go to them. Jesus taught this in the Sermon on the Mount: "If you are offering your gift at the altar and there remember that your brother has something against you, leave your gift there in front of the altar. First go and be reconciled to your brother; then come and offer your gift" (Matt. 5:23–24). You cannot enjoy fellowship with the Father, the Son, and the Holy Spirit when you know things are not right with others and you have not made an effort to put things right whether it involves a fellow Christian, an unsaved person, a relative, or one's spouse. As I said, you may not succeed. Total forgiveness is not necessarily reconciliation. But here is what I would ask you to consider:

1. If you owe money, pay it back—possibly even with interest.
2. If you have offended another person, apologize to them on bended knee.

Do not be defensive or make excuses. Ask for their forgiveness.

Totally forgiving oneself for some people, therefore, may call for making restitution. I would not want to play into someone's "overly scrupulous conscience" and have them push this too far. You are not going to get on with everybody, no matter how hard you try. Paul, however, said for us to try. He said it so reasonably: "If it is possible, as far as it depends on you, live at peace with everyone" (Rom. 12:18). Here is the principle that will faithfully be your guide and will not let you down: *do what makes for peace.* "Let us therefore make every effort to do what leads to peace and to mutual edification" (Rom. 14:19). The peace is both external (making amends with others as needed) and internal (when you feel total ease in your heart that you have done all you can do). This principle will not fail you and could be the key for some to bring them totally to forgiving themselves.

Wouldn't it be ironic if this part of the book would be the key to your forgiving yourself?

Another irony you have probably picked up by now is that *true* guilt is the easiest to deal with, that is, if we truly feel ashamed before *God*. Confessing our sins to God means instant forgiveness (1 John 1:9). He doesn't want to "rub our noses in it." For God forgives us more readily than we forgive ourselves. He is more gracious than we are! If you can ascertain that it is true guilt plaguing you, not pseudoguilt, be of good cheer—your problem can be solved in moments!

It is pseudoguilt, not true guilt, that people often spend years getting over. If, however, a good counselor can show them how true guilt is provided for by the God of the Bible, their client can better see how to handle pseudoguilt. This is because our problem ultimately is theological. It is applying good theology that will help one deal not only with true guilt but also with pseudoguilt, which I hope you are beginning to see by now. It is pseudoguilt that is the most difficult to cope with—the key to forgiving ourselves when you reject it for the glory of God.

God has made a way for us to deal with true guilt. He has done this in basically two ways: objectively and subjectively, and the two must come together. The objective way God has dealt with true guilt is by sending His beloved Son, Jesus Christ, to die on the cross for our sins. Yes, God sent His Son into the world to *die on a cross for our sins*. There is no grander knowledge in the universe than this. Never let yourself get over it. God sent Jesus to die for us. God punished Jesus for what we did. Why? Because He was our substitute. All our sins were laid on Him as though He were the guilty person (Isa. 53:6). This is why the New Testament claims that He "bore our sins" (1 Pet. 2:24). The Bible in a nutshell is this: "For God so loved the world that he gave his one and only Son, that whoever believes in him shall not perish but have eternal life" (John 3:16).

The subjective way true guilt is dealt with is by acknowledging our guilt to God. All that Jesus did and suffered for us is of no value until we believe. The essential work of the Holy Spirit is to convict of sin (John 16:7–8). But the Holy Spirit never leaves us to wallow in shame before God; He also convicts of "righteousness," said Jesus, "because I am going to the Father, where you can see me no longer" (John 16:10). This means that Jesus would not only die on a cross but also rise from the dead and ascend to the Father's right hand. When we believe in our hearts that Jesus died and was raised from the dead, God counts us as *righteous in His eyes* (Rom. 10:9–10). He declares us just. This is because our sin has been paid for, and we are affirming God's way of dealing with our sins.

And *if* as Christians we fall, and there is nobody who does not come short of God's high standard, and we confess our sins, we have that sweet promise that "he is faithful and just to forgive us our sins and purify us from all unrighteousness" (1 John 1:9). This confession of sin, however, must not be a glib, perfunctory, cerebral admission of imperfection but a true sorrow for having sinned against God. True guilt is based on what you and I must answer for at the judgment seat of Christ: "For we must all appear before the judgment seat of Christ, that each one may receive what is due him for the things done while in the body, whether good or bad" (2 Cor. 5:10). The old hymn is true:

Trust and obey,
For there's no other way
To be happy in Jesus,
But to trust and obey.
   —John Henry Sammis and Daniel B. Towner[4]

Pseudoguilt can take years to deal with, but true guilt can be dealt with in moments, once we come clean with God and resolve from this day forward to please Him.

PART II

Why It Is So Hard to Forgive Ourselves

CHAPTER 4

GUILT, GRIEF, REGRET, AND REPENTANCE

Every one can master a grief but he that has it.
—WILLIAM SHAKESPEARE[1]

Jesus wept.
—JOHN 11:35

When Martha and Mary sent word to Jesus that His friend Lazarus was ill, they assumed that Jesus would stop what He was doing, come immediately to Bethany, and heal Lazarus. But He showed up four days after the funeral instead.

Mary and Martha were bewildered—and angry. When Jesus finally came to Bethany, they blamed Him for their brother's death, pointing their fingers at Him one at a time, saying, "If you had been here, my brother would not have died" (John 11:21, 32). Jesus had no pseudoguilt for arriving when He did. After all, His priority was to the Father (John 5:19). Jesus listened and did not moralize them. He knew they were in grief. Instead of making them feel guilty, He wept with them (John 11:35).

When we are in grief it is good to cry. If Jesus could cry, so can you and I. Some people, especially men, are afraid or ashamed to cry. But it is good to do this; there is often healing in tears. God does not want us to feel guilty; this is why He has provided a way to deal with guilt of any kind. In any case, when we are in grief we don't need to pretend we are not hurting. God completely understands. Furthermore, this is not necessarily a time for a "stiff upper lip"; it is rather a time to be broken and sad—truly a time to weep and mourn (Eccles. 3:4).

Could it be that you are in grief at this moment? Is it possible that this grief is mixed with a little guilt?

The aim of this book is to help you to forgive yourself whatever the cause of your pain, whether it be guilt, grief, or regret. As I proceed I must say, however, that you will not be able to make progress in this area if true guilt has not been dealt with—where sin is involved and God has been offended. But I must say it again: if you confess and repent of your sins (1 John 1:9), there is no valid room left for true guilt—only pseudoguilt.

I want to show further why we struggle with pseudoguilt and why it is so hard for us to forgive ourselves. But there are certain distinctions that need to be looked at before we proceed—distinctions between guilt, grief, and regret.

Why is this chapter important? We must identify our true feelings and call a spade a spade. For example, is it *guilt* we are feeling—or is it *grief*? Or could it be *regret*? Just because we regret something, or meet disappointment, does not mean we should feel guilty. As there is a distinction between true guilt and pseudoguilt, so too there is a distinction between guilt and grief. Some people confuse the two; they feel guilty when what they are really experiencing is not guilt but rather grief or simply regret.

EXAMPLES OF GRIEF

Grief is deep or intense sorrow. It usually sets in as a result of a severe loss—a loved one, a friend, a job, a house or apartment, or a severe change of situation as the result of illness, retirement, an accident, or a loss of income. Grief will be painful and can take a long time to get over. But it is possible to have grief without any guilt, although you may impose guilt on yourself, thereby making yourself feel guilty. But you should not do this. Let me give examples of grief without guilt:

- My mother died at the age of forty-three; I was only seventeen. Losing your mother is traumatic at almost any age, but to lose your mother when you are a teenager is extremely hard. The grief lasted for weeks, months, and years. I have even wondered if I have ever gotten over it. If I let myself, I can begin to feel the sorrow as though it were yesterday. I feel so sorry that my mother died so young, that my little sister (age two when my mother died) had to grow up without her natural mother. I think too of the pain it was for my dad. I have wished that my mother could see the good things that have happened to me over the years, especially that she could meet Louise. All this is grief; it is not guilt.

- I know what it is to be jilted—to be abruptly rejected or abandoned. My first girlfriend in a sense took my mother's place. I used to think of the verse regarding Isaac. When he found Rebekah he "was comforted after his mother's death" (Gen. 24:67). But my girlfriend jilted me for someone else. I took it hard; the pain lasted a good while. There was no guilt. It just hurt. I eventually got over it.

• When we returned to America after twenty-five years at Westminster Chapel, nothing seemed right. An English missionary who had lived in the Far East and retired to the UK warned us that we should expect a year or more before we settled into our home in Florida. I laughed her to scorn! But I was wrong. It took at least three years before we began to settle in. Grief had set in the moment we arrived. I had given up a great church, great friends, the challenge to prepare fresh sermons, and, last but not least, London. "When a man is tired of London, he is tired of life," said Samuel Johnson.[2] We found it difficult to watch news reports from London, especially when they showed scenes of Big Ben, Buckingham Palace, or those around Picadilly Circus. There was no guilt. Only grief.

• An airline pilot, a strong Christian, who had a six-figure income and also took his family on free flights all over the world was suddenly made redundant because his company went bankrupt and was purchased by another airline that did not need his services. He was out of a job and income. The grief that set in was immense. But there was no guilt involved.

• A schoolteacher in her fifties who was never ill a day in her life developed a problem that made her see a physician. In a matter of weeks it turned out that she had a chronic illness that left her incapacitated, immobile, and unable to work. All this came suddenly. She is now housebound and lonely. The grief is terrific, but there was no cause for guilt.

- A comfortable family in Tennessee was awakened by their house being shaken. The next thing they knew, the roof was blown off and the walls of their house fell. They were suddenly lucky to be alive. A tornado had swept through the area. They lost everything they had and without notice had no place to live. One can imagine the trauma they went through, but there was no guilt.

As I said, grief is deep or intense sorrow. In 2 Corinthians 2:5 Paul referred to grief three times: "If anyone has caused *grief*, he has not so much *grieved* me as he has *grieved* all of you" (emphasis added). It is commonly thought that Paul is referring to the same man whose sexual sin caused grief in the church (cf. 1 Cor. 5:1–5). The Greek used in this passage refers to pain in the soul that is connected with suffering. The man in Corinth who had sinned no doubt felt grief but also guilt. Thankfully he repented. But there was no guilt in the grief the church experienced; they did what they had to do, namely, to obey Paul's word and excommunicate this person from the membership.

A person therefore may endure grief when it has nothing to do with guilt. Mind you, a person who suffers great guilt is in grief. All who feel guilty grieve, but not all who grieve have true guilt as the cause.

When it comes to physical pain, we tend to look for relief, whether aspirin for a headache or a stronger tablet for greater pain. In our age medical science has made it possible for most people to experience minimal physical pain.

But there is no tablet that cures the pain of the soul. One might resort to alcohol or drugs to drown the pain, but pain of the soul will return when the drug or alcohol wears off.

It is sometimes God's will for the Christian to experience suffering for a while. Suffering and endurance build character. Paul said that it is given to us not only to believe but also "to suffer" for Christ's sake (Phil. 1:29) and that there are trials that are "destined" (1 Thess. 3:3). God has given us the promise that no trial is allowed to fall our way but what is "common to man. And God is faithful; he will not let you be tempted [Gr. *peirasmos* means either "trial" or "temptation"] beyond what you can bear. But when you are tempted [or tried], he will also provide a way out so that you can stand up under it" (1 Cor. 10:13).

When a trial comes, it is assumed that we will suffer. In other words, it hurts. God has allowed this. When suffering comes we may wish for a "pill" to give relief, but sometimes we are simply called to endure suffering (2 Tim. 2:3). All suffering that the Christian undergoes is with a purpose and therefore will do us good, not harm. Whatever the suffering is, it will work together for good (Rom. 8:28). But while it lasts, it hurts.

Paul referred to his "thorn in the flesh"—it must have been painful. It was sent from God, but it did not come because of sin in his life; rather, it came because he needed something to keep him from being conceited and admired too much (2 Cor. 12:7). The Greek word for "thorn" (*skolops*) refers to pain like getting stuck with a fishhook; it won't kill you, but it hurts a lot. God's disciplining us, which is the way we should regard all suffering according to Hebrews 12:7, is not pleasant but "painful" (Heb. 12:11, "grievous," KJV), the root Greek word being the same as in 2 Corinthians 2:5. Such words as *grief, pain, suffering,* and being *disciplined* or *chastened* all refer to the simple fact that *it hurts,* and such hurt refers to pain of the soul.

Therefore when a person endures this kind of grief, he or she may understandably seek out a friend, pastor, or counselor. But there is not a lot, if anything, one can do to help alleviate pain except to point out that *God allows this for a purpose.* This will help some people, but not all. There will always be those who demand a rational explanation *now.* There are also those who understandably do not want to endure any kind of pain or grief—not even for a day or an hour. But Jesus reminded us that in this world "[we] will have trouble" (John 16:33). As Charles Colson put it, God does not promise to take us out of the fire, but He does promise to get into the fire with us.

Some people hastily assume that their pain, or even disappointment, is punishment from God. They therefore connect pain with guilt, thinking it is something they have done to cause this pain. God *can* do this; He may indeed roll up His sleeves and judge us. This was implied in the situation we saw above—2 Corinthians 2:5, which refers to the punishment given to the man in Corinth. This caused grief and pain for everybody. Sin was at the bottom of it. God stepped in and judged the man who sinned.

On the other hand, not all chastening is traceable to actual sin that we have committed. Chastening is essentially preparation—*not* God doing a "tit for tat" or getting even with us; He got even at the cross! "As far as the east is from the west, so far has he removed our transgressions from us" (Ps. 103:12). Chastening is meted out by a loving Father for this reason, "that we may share in his holiness...it produces a harvest of righteousness and peace for those who have been trained by it" (Heb. 12:10–11). God begins doing this early on in the life of the believer, not because of any sin committed but because we all need correction along the way.

It is possibly because some people hastily assume that any suffering, disappointment, or pain is owing to God being angry with them for past mistakes that they feel guilty when things go wrong.

There are those who feel guilty all the time, even before they get out of bed in the morning. This may be because of an excessively harsh parent who never approved of their son or daughter. I will have more to say about this later.

TOTAL FORGIVENESS

It is my opinion that the best remedy for any guilty feeling is totally forgiving *others*. I do you no favor not to put it like that. You may recall that the book you are reading is a sequel to my book called *Total Forgiveness*. There will no doubt be many who are reading the present book who have not read *Total Forgiveness*. Do not be overly concerned if you have not read my previous book. I simply have to say that forgiving ourselves is more easily done by those who have first forgiven *others*, and totally forgiving ourselves is more likely to take place when you have first totally forgiven everyone, anywhere, who has hurt you. It is almost an axiom: those who are hardest on themselves are hardest on others. And yet it is often true that you are not likely to forgive yourself until you have forgiven others. Therefore those who forgive others and let them off the hook will more likely forgive themselves.

Total forgiveness may be used interchangeably with what the apostle John calls "perfect love" (1 John 4:18). Perfect love is the same thing as the *agape* love described in 1 Corinthians, a key verse being that love "keeps no record of wrongs" (1 Cor. 13:5). The person who keeps no record of wrongs will never point the finger at anybody—directly or indirectly. For example, you won't say anything *to* the person that would make them feel uneasy or guilty by a barbed comment, nor will you say anything *about* another person that is unflattering and intended to make that person look bad. Such a judgmental word, whether it is cutting or even truthful, is almost always intended to ascribe guilt. When you totally forgive those who have hurt you, whether you regard them as enemies or people who have been not very nice, the result is that you will not make another feel guilty or even appear guilty. It is what John calls perfect love:

> There is no fear in love. But perfect love drives out fear, because fear has to do with punishment. The one who fears is not made perfect in love.
> —1 John 4:18

When you feel you are being punished by God, or when you want to punish another, it is probably because you have not yet totally forgiven others, yourself, or even God. Not that God has done anything wrong, far from it, but in our attitude there is a time when we must even forgive God for allowing something to happen that is painful. But we should not conclude that He allows this or that to happen because He is punishing us. As we will see later, that is exactly what the devil wants you to think. If you are governed by fear, it will be easy for Satan to make you think God is punishing you. Your weapon against the devil's accusation— I guarantee it—is total forgiveness. The devil is helpless in his effectiveness with you when you are without fear and bitterness.

Total forgiveness, then, is synonymous with perfect love, which casts out fear. You will have noticed in 1 John 4:18 that the apostle said that fear "has to do with punishment," a phrase we looked at in chapter 1. When you are governed by fear you:

1. Have not *felt* totally forgiven
2. Have not totally forgiven others (including God)
3. Have not totally forgiven yourself

The predictable result is that you may feel you are *being punished* by God. You may also want to punish someone else—to strike out at someone—even yourself. To summarize this thought in one sentence: if you have not totally forgiven those who have hurt you or have not totally forgiven yourself, you should not be surprised that you will feel a sense of *guilty grief* as if God were punishing you.

This kind of grief is unnecessary. God is *for* you—not against you! You should not forget that God knows your frame, knows your ability to cope, and always remembers that you are dust (Ps. 103:14). He is not unreasonable. He is not a tyrant. He is loving, merciful, and very tender (James 5:11). What He asks of you and me is not "burdensome" (1 John 5:3). If your aim is to please the Lord and you are walking in the light (1 John 1:7), you may be sure that any guilty grief—the wish to punish or the sense of being punished—is *not from God* and should not be allowed to grip you.

There can be guilt in grief, but I hope this book will help you to make the distinction—you will not suffer any guilt from grief. Grief hurts. But it is not always easy to get over grief, whether guilty grief or grief without guilt. Some unthoughtful person may moralize you for your feeling grief, but they have no idea what you may be going through. As Shakespeare put it, "Every one can master a grief but he that has it." Don't be intimidated by those who may shame you because you are sad. There will always be insensitive people who glibly say to you, "Get over it." They just don't understand. Grief is not easy to deal with, which is why Jesus wept with Martha and Mary. He shared their grief. The same Jesus who is the same yesterday, today, and forever (Heb.13:8) weeps with us, too.

Sometimes, however, there are people who grieve excessively over a person's death and feel great guilt, especially if they were not as good to the deceased as they should have been. Most clergymen will tell you that sometimes those who weep the most at a funeral or graveside and show the most emotion are those who hardly cared for the person when they were alive but now try to compensate for their failure by a lot of outward grief.

In any case, God does not want you to have grief that is traceable to *guilt*. You and I may have grief, pain, or disappointment because we are called to suffer at times. But it is not necessarily because God is punishing us. However, should it be that God *is* punishing us, as when our folly is exposed, we should take it with dignity and affirm God's wisdom and compassion. The man I referred to earlier in this book, the major church leader who was found to be living in immorality, has since stated that he is glad God brought it all out. I can believe that. If God judges us, it is because we are His own and because He isn't finished with us yet. As children of God we are in a win-win situation. If it is sin that causes grief, it means God is on our side and on our case and that He intends to work it out for good. If, however, no sin is at the bottom of our grief, which is better according to 1 Peter 3:17, it is because God has a wonderful plan for us.

You may ask: "How can I not feel guilty when God is disciplining me for my sin?" I reply: He does not discipline because He wants to make you feel worse, but because He wants you to feel affirmed—that He is on your case and that you are special. And should it be a severe judgment, as in the case of those who have openly brought disgrace upon Christ's name, I would plead with you, accept God's wisdom with dignity as did Eli, who knew God stepped in because of lack of care in his priestly responsibilities: "He is the LORD; let him do what is good in his eyes" (1 Sam. 3:18).

Regret

What about *regret*? We may regret things without imposing a painful guilt trip on ourselves. All of us have made mistakes; hence, we all have regrets. But it does not follow that we should beat ourselves black and blue because of past mistakes. There is pain in regret. But not necessarily guilt.

There is also pain without regret. Sometimes it is painful to make a hard decision, but it does not follow that you regret what you had to do. Paul said he was sorry he caused the Corinthians sorrow by his previous letter and was sorry over what he also had to do in the case of the wayward church member, but he added, "I do not regret it" (2 Cor. 7:8).

It is interesting that the word translated "regret" in 2 Corinthians 7:8 is from the Greek word *metamelomai*—the very same word used to describe the "repentance" of Judas Iscariot after he realized his fatal error by betraying Jesus (Matt. 27:3). The Greek word means "to experience remorse." It is precisely what Paul didn't feel when he stepped into the painful situation in Corinth. But regret and remorse were what Judas felt—too late. Unlike Paul, Judas must have experienced an incalculable measure of guilt. It is guilt that neither he nor anybody else could ever do anything about.

Think about those who, like Judas, will not go to heaven and will spend eternity in hell. One of the things that will make hell, hell will be the sense of guilt that will never go away. It is perhaps too awful to think about, but it has to be said nonetheless. I would be so pleased that a person came to Christ by reading this book, and sometimes a warning like this is what it takes for some. One of my predecessors at Westminster Chapel, Dr. G. Campbell Morgan, hardly known for being a hell-fire-and-brimstone preacher, actually said that his own experience in preaching evangelistic sermons was that more people came to Christ through the preaching of eternal judgment than by any other approach to the gospel.

EXAMPLES OF REGRET WITHOUT GUILT

The person who is riddled with guilt day and night, before breakfast and after going to bed without doing anything wrong whatsoever, probably has a psychological problem this book cannot help much with. But one who can look squarely at a situation that *could* make one feel guilty but realize that guilt in certain cases is ridiculous, just maybe one can start to make progress. Here are some examples of having sincere regret but no guilt whatsoever:

- A busy person receives a lot of e-mails and letters by regular mail but cannot possibly answer them all. He or she regrets this but feels no guilt.

- I myself took a pastorate in Ohio in 1962. We stayed there for eighteen months. It was a disaster. It was probably the unhappiest time of my life. I regret going but don't feel guilty that I went. Romans 8:28 is always true.

- A physician makes a wrong diagnosis, only going by the patient's symptoms and what appeared to be diagnostically correct. This is regrettable, but there is no cause of guilt since he followed what virtually all doctors would have done. However, had the doctor been hasty in his diagnosis, it would be different.

- Louise remembers how she missed what was probably the greatest service we had during our three years at Lauderdale Manors Baptist Church in Fort Lauderdale, Florida (1967–1970). Two unrelated people that many were praying for were gloriously converted the same evening. Louise regrets not being there but felt no guilt because our son, TR, was sick and she had to stay with him.

- I recently left in good time to get on a flight at the Miami airport. There was an accident on the road, and traffic was held up for two hours. I missed the plane and was late for the next meeting. I regretted this but refused to feel guilty about it. But had I left for the airport at the last minute, that would be different.

- I regretted that I had to come off a particular board of a well-known Christian organization. I had to cut down on activities, and it was a hard decision. Those in the organization were a bit hurt that I resigned, but I felt no guilt at all that I made the decision.

- For some reason I double-booked an engagement. I regretted that I found this out too late!

All regret is too late! There is no other kind of regret. Mistakes and misunderstandings are going to happen in this life. We all have twenty-twenty hindsight vision. There are, of course, degrees of regret, but you should learn to *refuse to feel guilty* when there was no harm intended. But if there is carelessness, that is different.

Remember Judas Iscariot. For him there was no hope. But there is hope for you and me if it is *metanoia* at work in us. This is the main word in the New Testament translated "repentance," which means "change of mind." It is one thing to regret, which Judas felt, and quite another to be given unfeigned repentance—a change of mind—which Judas was not given. When God grants you true repentance, it is cause for great rejoicing.

It takes no grace to regret; it takes grace to repent, for such a change of mind is a gift of God. The worse thing that can happen to a person is being unable to be renewed to repentance (Heb. 6:6). But don't worry! If there is a genuine change of mind in you that is God-ward, that you can hear the voice of the Holy Spirit and walk in the light God gives you, there is no valid basis to feel the pain of regret. Nor is there a need to think you are one of those who cannot be renewed again to repentance. Why? Because you know when God *has* granted repentance, which means that He is at work in you and will cause all things to work together for good (Rom. 8:28).

As for grief over the loss of a loved one, wasted years, missed opportunity, bad judgment, injuring a person in an accident, or missing a flight when it was crucial to be on time, grief or pain is inevitable. But it is not sin that caused it. You should not feel guilty.

Remember this: when there is no unconfessed sin involved, God does not want you to feel guilty. When you have confessed your sin to Him, there is no valid basis for guilt. *God does not want you to feel guilty.* That is why He wants you to forgive yourself. That is why He has given us Romans 8:28, a verse to which I keep referring—that all things work together for good.

By the way, there was a reason that Jesus did not heal Lazarus and turned up after the funeral. He thought raising Lazarus from the dead was a better idea than keeping him from dying! (See John 11:38–44.) When we are tempted to blame God for not showing up on time or for His letting bad things happen, I urge you to give Him the benefit of the doubt—He has a reason for all He does and does not do.

CHAPTER 5

OUR TWIN SINS

I have not met a single man who was morally as good as I.

—LEO TOLSTOY

I basically think that when one meets one's maker, if I do, there won't be anything I've done that I need to be ashamed of. Nothing.

—ACTRESS JOAN COLLINS[1]

Self-pity is the voice of pride in the heart.

—JOHN PIPER[2]

The heart is deceitful above all things and beyond cure. Who can understand it?

—JEREMIAH 17:9

Question: is the difficulty we have in totally forgiving ourselves traceable to a psychological weakness, or is the problem spiritual? I reply: it is both, but it is fundamentally a spiritual issue. The proof that this problem is spiritual at bottom is that Jesus commanded us to forgive and pray for our enemies, thus making this a spiritual requirement for all who would inherit the kingdom of heaven (Matt. 5–7). If we have obeyed His command totally to forgive our enemies, we have unfinished business with Him if we have not totally forgiven ourselves.

But I hold that there are also psychological issues that should be addressed, so in this chapter I want not to overlook emotional weaknesses even though the problem is ultimately a spiritual one. Why? Because Jesus would not ignore your emotional weaknesses. I want to make it as easy as possible for you to forgive yourself. The same Jesus who commands you to love your enemies also comes to you with infinite compassion and tenderness; He will not break a bruised reed, which I believe you are (Matt. 12:20).

You will recall that our personalities are like tips of an iceberg; we see 10 percent of the person, but 90 percent, what we don't see but which contains the fuller explanation of why we are like we are, is submerged in the sea of our subconscious memories. Because of varying degrees of damaged emotions, some Christians grow more quickly than others, learn more quickly than others, but also, even though all are equally responsible to do so, forgive more quickly than others. This means that some people can forgive themselves more quickly than others. The issue in total forgiveness is ultimately spiritual, yes, but I equally know that our Lord is gracious and knows each of us backward and forward. As I have stated, Dr. Clyde Narramore taught me that "every person is worth understanding."

Consider the following situations:

- A young lady is sexually abused by her father from a very early age; she cannot remember a time when he did not abuse her—until she managed to leave home. But as often is the case, she blames herself and feels she must have done something to cause him to abuse her. She has forgiven her father, but she has trouble forgiving herself for all she did. Jesus would be patient and tender toward this girl.

- A young man, not brought up in a Christian home, was taught by his father to never forgive anybody who hurts him. This was drummed into him; one could almost call it brainwashing. He became a Christian and believes God has forgiven him all his sins, but he struggles to forgive himself for holding grudges over the years. He has sought to forgive people but feels so guilty that he takes so long to do so.

- A woman with low self-esteem has blamed herself all her life for her failure to please her father, failure to get a university degree, failure to get a better job, and failure to find a husband. She struggles to forgive herself for not having a happier life.

- A medical student, a Christian, feels guilty that he is not attracted to women but only men. He accepts the biblical teaching on this matter but cannot forgive himself for his sexual orientation. He cannot remember a time when he was any different.

- A medical student, a Christian, says that her father drove her to being the "best" in the class. She was always that, got a "first" in university, then became a doctor, and after that a consultant. She has difficulty having a good relationship with either sex; she is so "high powered" that people are intimidated by her. She blames herself that she cannot make friends.

- A Christian lady who has been clinically diagnosed as manic depressive (now sometimes called bipolar) has her swings of mood; when she has a "down" she feels guilty for this and asks for prayer. She was rejected by both her parents and never felt accepted by them—or anybody else. The psychological blueprint for her is part of the explanation for her struggle to forgive herself when she goes through a time of depression.

- A man who came to Christ through our street-witnessing program at the Chapel (called Pilot Lights) struggled to be accepted. His mother put him out to be adopted at an early age. But his adopted parents rejected him when he was a teenager. After he became a Christian, he decided to look up his natural mother. She did not want to talk with him. He then went to his adopted parents. They told him to leave and never come back. He blamed himself for all this and feels guilty that he struggles to forgive himself.

Not only is every person worth understanding, but we all also have a story to tell. When I consider my own family background and upbringing, I regard it as utterly sublime compared to many stories I have heard. And whereas we all have a mandate to forgive others and totally forgive ourselves, God is gracious, merciful, and understands us when we struggle with our emotional baggage. A verse I never tire of quoting is: God knows our frame and "remembers that we are dust" (Ps. 103:14).

Let me tell you one reason I think I have had trouble forgiving myself. My old church in Ashland, Kentucky, taught a doctrine known as sinless perfection. Perhaps not all the ministers in that denomination emphasized this, but my own pastor certainly did.

And my dad bought the whole package and brought me up on it. If I am honest, I am still plagued by it to some degree to this very day, and I have to watch out for it all the time. My former teaching required me to be sinlessly perfect, and my father required that I perform well in school—making all As on my report card. This set me up to be very self-righteous, judgmental, and hard on myself. And yet I know I did not spend time as I should with our children, missing many opportunities to spend precious moments with them. Although we had a reasonably good ministry at Westminster Chapel, I never saw what I hoped would be accomplished during my time there. And, despite my belief in the sovereignty of God, I tended to blame myself that we did not have greater blessing. I have since accepted things as they were, getting the victory over pseudoguilt, and now believe that I accomplished what God intended during my twenty-five years there.

SELF-RIGHTEOUSNESS

Although it is not so easy to see at first, one of the main spiritual reasons we often cannot forgive ourselves is self-righteousness. By nature we are blind not only to our sinfulness, but also especially to self-righteousness and why it is so displeasing to God. Self-righteousness is that innate assumption in us that says we are sufficiently good in ourselves. We have no need for anyone to atone for us; we can atone for sin by our good works. I'm sorry, but you don't need to have any particular kind of background—cultural, theological, or educational—to learn how to be self-righteous. We are *all* self-righteous—including you! It is the way we were from our mother's womb, inheriting Adam's and Eve's depravity—including their refusal to take the blame for their sin (Gen. 3:9–13; Ps. 51:5).

In the case of Job, self-righteousness was the last thing he saw about himself, but it probably was one of the main things God wanted him to see about himself! At the beginning of the Book of Job it is said that he was "blameless and upright; he feared God and shunned evil" (Job. 1:1). When God gave Satan permission to test Job, Job did well at first—he was truly off to a good start: "In all this, Job did not sin by charging God with wrongdoing" (Job 1:22). But after that God put the heat on Job, allowing the devil more latitude. Before long Job cursed the day of his birth—not something that pleases the Lord (Job 3:1). Then came his "friends" who mercilessly hammered him with questions and accusations, claiming that there must be sin in Job's life or God would not have allowed such trouble. In all Job's protestations, he completely lost self-control in the end, and the depth of his heart was eventually openly manifest— his self-righteousness (Job 32:1). In the meantime he said to these "friends," "I will never admit you are in the right. . . . I will maintain my righteousness and never let go of it" (Job 27:5–6).

It took a long time before Job climbed down and said to the Lord, "I am unworthy—how can I reply to you? I put my hand over my mouth" (Job 40:4), and then he repented in "dust and ashes" (Job 42:6). Self-righteousness is the last thing we tend to see in ourselves, not realizing how heinous it is in God's eyes. And yet we *never will* see it in ourselves unless God intervenes—as He did in the case of Job.

Righteous people need to see their self-righteousness. I know a lot of so-called "good" people—great examples of holy living insofar as their being outwardly blameless is concerned. They are, for all practical purposes, sinless in that they, like the Pharisees in Jesus's day, do not outwardly break any of the Ten Commandments. The trouble is, so many people like this assume that their righteousness is what gives them an entrance to heaven. The sobering thing about such people is that they are still unconverted, for they are trusting their own good works rather than Christ's blood and righteousness on their behalf. They do not have a "sense" of sin that comes when they examine themselves before God or in the light of Jesus's interpretation of the Law, neither do they see that their righteous acts are like "filthy rags" in God's sight (Isa. 64:6).

It is only the Holy Spirit who will help you and me to see that we are guilty sinners and need the atoning grace of the Lord Jesus Christ to make it to heaven. We are by nature loath to trust His blood to wash away our guilty past. Furthermore, just because we become Christians, it does not follow that we have no self-righteousness left in us. Quite the contrary! It is something we must guard against all our lives.

Not only that, but we are naturally *afraid* to forgive ourselves because (we tell ourselves) we are responsible for our past. Even though we know we are forgiven by Him, we still often fear that God would surely require us to bear the weight of what we have done. The devil would make us think this, too. "It is great," we keep telling ourselves, "that all my sins are forgiven, but God expects me to feel guilty forever and ever for what I have done."

So there we go again (should this scenario describe you) thinking that God is still punishing us! The devil tells us it is irresponsible of us not to have to face our folly and simply pass the buck to God in order to let us get away with what we did. That seems unfair. But it is our pride, with Satan's goading, making us think like this. God's letting us totally off the hook also seems too good to be true. "Surely," we tell ourselves, "I must not let myself totally off the hook; I must at least partly pay—atone, compensate, make up—for my shameful mistakes. I surely don't deserve to forgive myself totally in one stroke just because Jesus died for me. There must be more," we keep saying to ourselves, "that I must do before I can lean wholly on Jesus's blood. It does not seem *just* that I get away with my failure—as easy as that!"

But God says it *is* just. He uses that very word! "If we confess our sins, he is faithful and *just* and will forgive us our sins and purify us from all unrighteousness" (1 John 1:9, emphasis added). That means God, whose essential nature is love and justice, has thought it through and decreed to declare Himself *just*—fair, righteous, legally right—to forgive us.

It is for this very reason that we are required to forgive ourselves—because God says so. How can it bless Him, bring Him honor and glory, when He forgives us but we don't forgive ourselves? It is like a slap in His face! Not only that, but if He forgives us and we don't forgive ourselves, we are—even if involuntarily—competing with His way of providing forgiveness, as if to put down His method, if not also questioning His integrity and justice. That is not good to do! But God has given us the *gospel*—a word that simply means "good news"—that all our sins have been fully paid for by the death of His Son. Total forgiveness is an offer, and we have not fully accepted the package if we don't forgive ourselves—totally.

Yes, it does seem too good to be true. The gospel is *always* too good to be true!

> It is a thing most wonderful,
> Almost too wonderful to be,
> That God's own Son should come from heaven
> And die to save a child like me.
> —W. W. How[3]

We all need to see the subtlety of self-righteousness and how it is a part of us and we are not aware of it. We need also to see the danger of it, how it is very obnoxious in God's sight. This is scary. This means that not forgiving ourselves is to our peril. It is also the greatest obstacle to true spirituality. Self-righteousness is the easiest sin to see in others but the hardest to see in ourselves. This is what caused Isaiah to say, "Woe to me!" (Isa. 6:5). It was his blindness to self-righteousness that horrified him.

Self-righteousness is what makes us judgmental, causing us to point the finger. It is what makes us defensive, argumentative, and smug. Smugness is a feeling of well-being by which we don't think, we *know* we've got it right and are a cut above others! God hates it. It is what described the church at Laodicea (Rev. 3:14–18).

Perhaps the most dangerous thing about self-righteousness is its blinding power—both to the gospel and the truth about ourselves. Sometimes a blatant murderer or serial adulterer will see nothing wrong in what they do (Prov. 14:12). Why? Self-justification, which springs from self-righteousness, sets in as quickly as their evil acts. Imagine, too, saying that no one is morally as good as you are! Would you say this about yourself? Surely not! Imagine also a person willing to meet their Maker and feeling there is nothing they have ever done wrong!

Self-righteousness therefore is what keeps us from having objectivity about ourselves. It militates against faith, because by nature we opt for approval before God by our works. However, once the scales fall from our eyes we are amazed that we could have been so confident in ourselves. This is why it requires the Holy Spirit to make us see the truth about the gospel and ourselves.

What is more, when you are self-righteous, it is what will not allow you to forgive yourself. You may not realize it at first, but I have to tell you, self-righteousness is competing with God. It is playing "one-upmanship" with God, as if suffering guilt for your own sin is better than His way of providing atonement, even if unconsciously, claiming that you know better than He does as to the way forward! The devil will do all he can to keep you from totally forgiving yourself by accepting God's total forgiveness.

I can make you a promise: when you see the truth of self-righteousness, you will gladly step aside, stop punishing yourself, and thank God for the blood of Jesus that forgives all your past, no matter how bad it was. He says gently but firmly to you right now: "Forgive yourself. *I* have forgiven you. Does *My* opinion matter? If so, forgive yourself." Doing this is what pays greatest respect for the blood Jesus shed on the cross two thousand years ago. Do you not want to show highest honor for the blood of Jesus? Then forgive yourself!

Self-Pity

But self-righteousness has a twin—self-pity. We saw that Job eventually saw that he was self-righteous. But parallel with this sin was his self-pity: "Although I am blameless, I have no concern for myself; I despise my own life" (Job 9:21). "I wish I had died before any eye saw me" (Job 10:18). "Who can see any hope for me?" (Job 17:15). "God has wronged me and drawn his net around me" (Job 19:6). "Oh, for the days when I was in my prime.... Young men saw me and stepped aside and the old men rose to their feet.... But now they mock me, men younger than I" (Job 29:4, 8; 30:1).

Elijah, one of the most spectacular prophets in the Old Testament, was filled with self-pity. He wanted to die! Why? Believe it or not, it was because he was "no better" than his ancestors (1 Kings 19:4). Why should this bother him? Who ever said he *was* better than those who preceded him? Who ever required that he be better than those who went on before? The answer is, Elijah imposed a standard and a wish upon himself that God did not put there. He wanted to be the best there ever was! Yes, we are talking about the great Elijah—a man who, according to James, was "just like us" (James 5:17). He had a rival spirit with previous great men in history. His pride was at the bottom of it all. He also thought he was the only true prophet of God alive—he was wrong about that as well. (See 1 Kings 18:13.) God eventually but tenderly pointed out to him that there were seven thousand who had not bowed the knee to Baal (1 Kings 19:18).

Jacob, examined in more detail later in chapter 7, was full of self-pity. Even when he was presented before King Pharaoh he could only mope before his majesty and regret that he was only one hundred thirty years old! "My years have been few and difficult, and they do not equal the years of the pilgrimage of my fathers" (Gen. 47:9). Like Elijah, he compared himself to those who preceded him and lamented that he did not match them.

Self-pity is feeling sorry for yourself. You may not see it at first, but self-pity is not only selfish but also anger toward God. We feel sorry for ourselves because God allowed a situation to happen that makes no sense. So we blame Him but continue to remain full of self-pity. We feel sorry for ourselves because God seems to have deserted us and there seems no way out. We feel sorry for ourselves that we were so stupid. We got ourselves into this mess; we must get ourselves out of it. This shows that, as Dr. John Piper has observed, pride is at the bottom of self-pity. It is the twin sin to self-righteousness.

Self-pity is sulking before God, almost demanding that He either explain Himself or immediately step in. But self-pity gets us nowhere with God: "For the wrath of man worketh not the righteousness of God" (James 1:20, KJV). You may try shaking your fist at Him, yelling at Him, accusing Him. You will not get one word back. It does not even begin to move Him. He takes no notice. There is nothing more counterproductive than self-pity.

And yet self-pity is also a fruit of pseudoguilt, imposing guilt on ourselves that God did not put there. It seems so right at first; our feeling sorry for ourselves seems quite normal and right. "Who could feel otherwise given my situation?" we tell ourselves.

Self-pity, like self-righteousness, then, is always counterproductive; it doesn't do any good; it gets us nowhere. It never achieves its goals; we only hurt ourselves. Foolishly we tell ourselves that we don't deserve Christ's atonement, that we are so pitiful and unworthy, and that we should pay for our own sin. Therefore self-pity, like its twin, will lead us *away* from totally forgiving ourselves by trusting Christ's blood, and it will make us wallow in our sorry state indefinitely.

We all have given in to this. At least I know I have. It is natural to feel sorry for yourself. No grace from God is needed to bring you to self-pity. It takes the grace of God, however, to wake us up and cause us to snap out of it.

Coming out of self-pity is a choice we have to make. If you are not careful, the devil will keep you there. He does not want you to forgive yourself.

In the same way, you must make a choice to forgive yourself totally by affirming the blood of the Lord Jesus Christ—and never look back. God wants you to be free.

Don't let the sins of self-righteousness and self-pity deprive you of peace, joy, and freedom—which are rightfully yours! Your sins have been forgiven—all of them, however horrible, inexcusable, and wicked. And be careful—self-righteousness is a sin in the sight of God and just as evil in His eyes as any gross wickedness is in yours!

Know equally that we have a wonderful heavenly Father. His mercy endures forever. He sent His Son to be tempted and tried "just as we are" (Heb. 4:15). He therefore does not moralize us, He does not shame us, He never rejects us, and He always is touched with the feeling of our weaknesses.

None of us is perfect. None of us had perfect parents. None of us had perfect backgrounds. We all have our scarred emotions.

Forgiving ourselves, however, is our responsibility. It is for our good. We who do it are the winners! Those who don't forgive themselves forfeit the tranquil liberty that belongs to them. Most of all, forgiving ourselves pleases God. There is no greater joy or satisfaction than that.

Don't you be among those who forfeit that satisfaction. That is what Satan wants you to do.

CHAPTER 6

OUR GREAT ACCUSER, THE DEVIL

Now have come the salvation and the power and the kingdom of our God, and the authority of his Christ. For the accuser of our brothers, who accuses them before our God day and night, has been hurled down. They overcame him by the blood of the Lamb and by the word of their testimony; they did not love their lives so much as to shrink from death.

—REVELATION 12:10–11

For our struggle is not against flesh and blood, but against the rulers, against the authorities, against the powers of this dark world and against the spiritual forces of evil in the heavenly realms.

—EPHESIANS 6:12

And though this world,
With devils filled,
Should threaten to undo us,
We will not fear,
For God hath willed,
His will to triumph through us.

The prince of darkness grim,
We tremble not for him.
His rage we can endure,
For, lo, his doom is sure;
One little word shall fell him.

—MARTIN LUTHER[1]

God does not want you to feel guilty. But Satan does. Making you feel guilty could almost be called his "job description."

Therefore, as we have seen a number of times already, one of the reasons you have difficulty forgiving yourself is that Satan is working behind the scenes day and night. His chief weapon: accusing you, making you feel guilty, telling you how bad you are, how unworthy and how stupid you are to believe God's promises. That is his job. Never forget it.

The purpose of this chapter is to help you to see what Satan is up to—and not let him succeed with you.

I want to make some general observations about the devil—what I think you need to know if you are struggling to forgive yourself. There are two cautions before I proceed:

1. Don't think that you should become an "expert" on the devil. Those who have this aspiration are not in my opinion truly mature Christians. Indeed, people like this are often the ones who get in over their heads and are overcome, like the sons of Sceva. (See Acts 19:13–16.)

2. You do need, however, the ABCs knowledge of his ways. Paul could say, "We are not unaware of his

schemes" (2 Cor. 2:11), "not ignorant of his devices" (KJV).

For the purposes of this book, here is how I would describe his ways:

1. He would prefer that you believe he does not exist. Unbelief in the devil is the devil's work. If you don't believe in the reality of Satan, you have just told me he has succeeded with you.

2. If you do believe he exists, he then wants to dominate your thinking; he will want you to think about him all the time—and make you afraid of him. Always bluffing, he will intimidate you and make you think he is all-powerful. He is not; when compared to almighty God, he is a weakling but is still given limited authority on this planet for a limited time. Some people in their fear of the devil's power give the impression that they ascribe more credit to Satan than to God.

3. He is always under God's sovereign thumb; he can proceed no further than what God allows (Job 1–2). Therefore know that the buck stops with God. Whatever trial you are going through, never forget that God gave Satan permission before He let him have a go at you. God knows you are big enough for it or He would not have let it happen (1 Cor. 10:13).

4. Satan is a liar (John 8:44). Sometimes, however, he will quote Scripture (Matt. 4:6). But as the Puritan William Perkins used to say, "Don't believe the devil,

even when he tells the truth!" Some of his accusations concerning you will be true. He will throw up your past. It is essential to remember about Satan that all he does is to work against the interests of Jesus Christ, his archenemy, who is the embodiment of *truth* as much as Satan is the embodiment of *lie*.

5. His main tactic insofar as the Christian is concerned is to accuse. His manner is the quintessential example of pointing the finger. He keeps a record of wrongs, has a memory better than yours, and will remind you of things you thought you had forgotten. He has one goal: to bring you down and keep you from pure joy. Remember, *he does not want you to forgive yourself.*

6. He is resistible. He will come on to you like a roaring lion, making you think you are defeated before you have had a chance to count to ten (1 Pet. 5:8). This is an example how he will lie to you. But you are to resist him. He will make you think he is irresistible—that is a lie. Resist him, and you will find out! The proof he is a weakling is that he has to flee once he sees you are on to him.

7. Spiritual warfare is essentially *defensive*. This means that you must *not* go on the attack. Attacking him is foolish. I know too many stories of people who were going to "have a go" at Satan. Some today have lost their ministries because they promoted themselves to the level of their incompetence—attacking Satan. You have no promise that he will flee when you attack him,

only when he attacks *you*. This is so important that
I will return to it below.

One of the more disquieting aspects of modern Christianity in
some places is the high profile given to the devil and "spiritual
warfare." One gets the impression sometimes that all things that
go against our will are of the devil. He gets more attention than
God sometimes! Most of all, I wonder if some people fear the devil
more than they do God.

One of my favorite lines from Martin Luther's hymn, quoted
at the beginning of this chapter is: "For, lo, his doom is sure, *one
little word* shall fell him." Luther had many battles with the devil.
I suspect the devil was very threatened indeed by him. Luther was
not the slightest bit afraid of the devil.

I would not want you to be naïve or unaware of the devil's
power, however. My dad used to say to me that the devil is "very
crafty, second only to God in power and wisdom." Yes. Quite. But
don't forget he is *second* to God, a far second and nowhere equal to
Him: "The one who is in you is greater than the one who is in the
world" (1 John 4:4). It is God to whom *he* answers, and it is God
to whom *we* answer. The buck stops with God.

It is interesting to me that Satan is called the "accuser of our
brothers" in Revelation 12:10. This phrase has been immense
comfort to the people of God over the centuries. Anybody who has
had any experience in the wiles of the devil can tell you this is his
chief tactic—to accuse. Two other things—quoted at the beginning of this chapter—that are incorporated in the way in which
Satan was defeated are:

1. The means by which he was overcome, namely, the
   blood of the Lamb

2. How the people of God were unashamed to confess faith
   in the blood of Jesus—"the word of their testimony"

In other words, it was not only the *blood* of Jesus that defeated
Satan, but it was also *faith* in Jesus's blood.

When Satan accuses you of your past, remind him that your
sins have been forgiven by God—through the shed blood of Jesus.
The most sublime lines in John Newton's hymn "Approach, My
Soul, the Mercy Seat" are these:

> Be Thou my Shield and hiding Place,
> That, sheltered by Thy side,
> I may my fierce accuser face,
> And tell him Thou hast died!
>
> —JOHN NEWTON[2]

Put all your eggs in one basket—the blood of Jesus. Don't point
Satan to your good works, your best efforts, your resolve to do
better, or the fact that you may have improved over the years. No,
don't do that. Point him to the blood of Jesus. Nothing more. Rest
your case there. You know that you are a great sinner, but you have
a great God and a great Savior, and all your sins are washed away
by Jesus's blood. That is what Revelation 12:11 means by the *word
of your testimony.* You can sing along with another great hymn:

> My hope is built on nothing less
> Than Jesus' blood and righteousness.
> I dare not trust the sweetest frame,
> But wholly lean on Jesus' name.
>
> —EDWARD MOTE[3]

We are talking about how to deal with true guilt, where you have sinned against God, whether in the distant past or recent past. And should it be that your pseudoguilt went on too long so that it too crossed over a line and became a sin, then confess that, too! Don't give the devil a crumb! My word to you: *so believe in the blood of Jesus* to satisfy God's demands that *His* satisfaction is all that matters to you.

Here is what will follow: the devil will flee and leave you alone for a season. And should he come back an hour or a day later and accuse you of the same sin or a different one, your weapon is the same—the blood of Jesus. It doesn't get better than that; don't try to improve on that. Satan fears any man and any woman who so believes in the blood of Jesus to wash away sin that he will be less and less likely to raise the subject so often.

We are not talking about enacting a repetitive formula, merely saying, "The blood of Jesus...the blood of Jesus...the blood of Jesus"—although I don't discount that. The important thing is that you so *believe* that the blood of Christ is God's idea and way of dealing with sin that the *word of your testimony* is what makes the blood "work" for you, if I may put it that way. Your faith *ratifies* Christ's blood, which means you consent to what the blood means to God so that it takes effect. Satan will depart, not unlike a dog with his tail tucked between his legs.

THE THREE RS OF SPIRITUAL WARFARE

And what if Satan keeps hounding you? I must now introduce to you the three Rs of spiritual warfare:

1. Recognize
2. Refuse
3. Resist

I am indebted to Dr. Harry Kilbride for this lovely insight in a sermon I heard him preach many years ago. I have never forgotten it.

Recognize

This means to recognize whether it is the devil indeed that is behind these thoughts you are having. It is not always easy to know that it is the devil when you have a particular thought. You might think it is God, and know, too, that it can be your own thought. If you have a tendency to daydream or fantasize very much, you will probably have thoughts all the time that come neither from God nor the devil. So be aware of this, should this be a weakness of yours. It is possible to have thoughts that come immediately from yourself—quite apart from God or the devil. If you are a bit melancholy by temperament or if you have a tendency to depression, you may have negative thoughts quite often. Try to understand that these thoughts come from inside of you and therefore may have nothing to do with the devil's accusations. It could be that you keep accusing yourself! But know also that the devil can exploit your weaknesses, put thoughts into your head, and mislead you.

Do not forget that Satan can masquerade as "an angel of light" (2 Cor. 11:14). The best of God's people are sometimes deceived for a while (Matt. 24:24). In the early church there were false prophets around, and it was not always easy to detect who was true and who was false (1 John 4:1). There are also well-meaning people who might also be described as "busybodies"—who can give you a heavy feeling by their being nosey. The devil can use people like this.

So how do you recognize that it is Satan and not God who is giving you certain thoughts? Here is how to know it is the devil and *not* God:

1. When you feel "put down" or demoralized. God would never do that. Jesus never did that. A bruised reed He will not break (Matt. 12:20). Whenever you feel hurt or less than respected by a word or thought that comes into your head, it is the devil.

2. When you feel oppressed. I remind you of what Dr. Martyn Lloyd-Jones used to teach me: "God never oppresses us." This was so emancipating for me. When a spirit of heaviness hovers over you, mark it down: it is not God doing this—it is the devil.

3. When you feel "got at." That is the accuser at work. You will say, "But doesn't God do that with us?" No. When you feel "got at," you are sad, hurt, and singled out as unclean—that is the devil. When God speaks to you, it will be a feeling of being affirmed and of hope, and He will show you a way forward.

4. When there is no positive way forward. Let us say that you are given a word or thought that not only is unhelpful but also leaves you without any remedy. When there is no remedy provided in the word that comes to you, this I can only call "vintage Satan." He never shows a way forward; he only wants to keep you feeling that there is nothing you can do. Satan loves to lead people down cul-de-sacs. That is one of the things he does best.

5. When the result of the thought that comes to you puts you in bondage. Satan loves to keep us bound—unable to move freely (Luke 13:16). He does that with our spirit, giving us an inner feeling of bondage and

immobility. When you cannot forgive yourself, you are sometimes almost immobile—at least internally. You are unmotivated and unable to get things done. You are devoid of expectancy and aspiration. That is exactly where Satan wants you.

On the other hand, when God comes there will be joy and liberty: "Where the Spirit of the Lord is, there is freedom" (2 Cor. 3:17). This is as opposite to the devil's work as you can get. You will never be demoralized by the Holy Spirit—even when He shows you your sin. This is because the way He does it gives us hope; He convicts us, shows the way forward, points us to the blood of Jesus, lets us save face, and sets us free.

How does the devil speak to us? Basically two ways:

1. By putting thoughts into your head when you are alone
2. Through another person's comments

Yes, he may attack you when you are utterly alone. Although he does not know exactly what you are thinking, he knows your temperament and weakness. And though he does not know what is on your mind at a given moment, he knows what *he* puts there and can tell if you are taking it or rejecting it.

When you are alone

I know what it is to have a quiet time, praying and reading my Bible. Then all of a sudden comes a rather oppressive thought. "Where did that come from?" I ask myself. Then I realize, "*I* did not come up with that; *God* did not come up with that. That was the devil." When I come to terms with that, I refuse to give any time or dignity to the idea that came to me. And guess what? The oppression vanishes as quickly as it started.

You may ask, "But can't we give ourselves thoughts that are not good?" Yes. But if you dwell on them you risk inviting Satan to enter into your thought life after all. Make it a rule: *refuse to think about things that oppress you.* Here is your verse: "Whatever is true, whatever is noble, whatever is right, whatever is pure, whatever is lovely, whatever is admirable—if anything is excellent or praiseworthy—think about such things" (Phil. 4:8). Someone will say, "Yes, but it is *true* that I have made such a mess of my life, and how can I not think about it?" I reply: because God isn't finished with you yet. That is why He reminds you of the blood of Jesus. The blood of Jesus cleansing from all sin means *there is a future* out there to be lived. The blood of Christ always means a new beginning.

Another person's comments

The second way the devil speaks is through another person. That individual may say something that is intentionally hurtful. The positive point here is that is an easy way to tell it is the devil! You know that this person is not speaking for God; they are wanting to hurt you. Jesus does not do that. I know it is not easy, but try not to let an unhelpful or hurtful comment do for you what Satan wants it to accomplish. Don't give him that joy!

And if the person is throwing up your past or saying things over which you have no control, remember that Jesus is standing very near you. He knows what is happening and fully understands. Pour your heart out to Him. Let the attack be a major victory for you.

Rule of thumb: Satan always overreaches himself. The only exception to that is when you give him a bit of dignity by listening to him and taking him seriously. But when you refuse to be discomforted by evil thoughts, you will see—perhaps sooner rather than later—that God will use this incident as a milestone in your life to bring you closer to Him. I have had it happen to me a thousand times.

Sometimes, however, a person may not intend to hurt you, but you *hear* something they did not mean. The devil will exploit that, knowing your frame and weakness as he does. When that happens, learn not to take the remark personally; see it as the devil's way to bring you down at an unexpected moment.

By the way, there is a way of *guaranteeing* that Satan will invariably overreach himself. It is when you walk in total forgiveness, including forgiving yourself. I promise you! If you walk in total forgiveness (you can trust this word to the hilt), Satan will overreach himself every single time he attacks you. What is more, you will be miles ahead as a result of his attack, and probably in a very short period of time.

Refuse

This is the second R in spiritual warfare. This has been mentioned already. It simply means that you *refuse to dwell on the thought he puts into your head*. The moment you have concluded, "This is the devil, not God," your next move is to refuse to give any time to the thought.

What the devil wants to see is how bothered you are by the accusation. When he throws a fiery dart (Eph. 6:16) at you, he wants it to "stick" so that you feel the pain of it for a long time. It is better, of course, to see the attack coming so you can put the shield of faith up in advance. But this is not always possible. He often manages to get a cutting word to us—and we feel the pain. But the pain will go away when you refuse to dwell on it.

Since our retirement I was given a broadside attack in a book review. What was said was not even true. But it hurt. I had one of two choices: to dwell on it and start feeling sorry for myself that people would read this and believe it, or *refuse to dwell* on what the writer said. I chose the latter. I promise you, it stopped hurting at once! And when I do think of it, which I do once in a while, I let myself have a good laugh. The devil doesn't want that!

Sometimes, however, Satan ruthlessly attacks us in the middle of the night, either through dreams or through thoughts that keep us awake. This is hard. I struggle here. When I am tired and vulnerable in the middle of the night, it is often difficult to think clearly and act in the manner that I know is right. Satan never plays fair! All one can do is plead for the mercy of God, who enables us to find grace in the time of need (Heb. 4:16).

I was privileged to meet Oral Roberts not long ago. He invited Louise and me into his home. I wanted to thank him for his commendation of my book *Total Forgiveness*. We got to talking about sleep and getting enough sleep. He counseled me to do what I have heard before, but it was so timely: start quoting Scripture! When you do that, the devil flees—and you go back to sleep.

The point is, once you recognize the devil as being the culprit for your being "down" or "low," *refuse* him with all your might. Get out an old hymnal and read through the hymns—or sing them! Or turn to a good book. Mrs. Martyn Lloyd-Jones once shared a problem she used to have and how Satan would bring this fear before her. She told me she learned to "refuse to think about it." "Just start thinking about anything else," she would say to me. "Anything else."

Resist

This is the third R in spiritual warfare. You will recall that I stated above that all spiritual warfare is *defensive*. This is extremely important. You are never called to go on the offensive in combating Satan, unless it means that you march into his territory to preach the gospel. That is different. We are all called to go into the world to preach the gospel (Mark 16:15). Furthermore, any obedience to God will offend the devil.

However, I lovingly warn you: if you attack Satan, like some who want to "give a go" at the devil, you are in a perilous situation. I repeat: you have no promise that he will flee when you go on the attack, but you have a wonderful promise that he will flee when he attacks *you*. The term *resist* is found in two places in the New Testament:

Resist the devil, and he will flee from you.

—James 4:7

Your enemy the devil prowls around like a roaring lion looking for someone to devour. Resist him, standing firm in the faith.

—1 Peter 5:8–9

You will note the word *standing* in 1 Peter 5:9. This is a very important word for you to remember when it comes to resisting the devil. You are required to *stand*. In the most famous spiritual warfare passage in the New Testament, the word *stand* is found four times:

Put on the full armor of God so that you can take your stand against the devil's schemes....Therefore put on the full armor of God, so that when the day of evil comes, you may be able to stand your ground, and after you have done everything, to stand. Stand firm then...

—Ephesians 6:11–14

To stand means what it says—to stand. You don't walk, you don't run, you don't crawl, you don't fall, and you don't go backward. You *stand*. That is all you are required to do. For standing is resisting. When you stand up against his attack, you are resisting. Your only job is to keep from moving, either by going forward, dropping behind, tripping, or falling.

To put it another way, when Satan attacks, don't try to make a lot of progress. Don't even move. Just stay put. *Resisting the devil is great progress when he attacks.* This is the way he overreaches himself. It is when you stand. You say, "Christ died for my sins." You may say, "Your accusations are true, but Jesus died and shed His blood for my sins."

There is one thing more you can do: forgive yourself. Make the decision to do it. It is something you must *choose* to do, not something you wait until you feel "led" to do it. You must do it *now*. Forgive yourself. Wherever you are as you read this very book—at home, on public transportation, on your lunch hour—wherever, do it now and resist the devil. On what authority? On the authority of God's Word. By what rationale? By the rationale that forgiving yourself is precisely the opposite of what Satan wants. Do the opposite of what you know he wants, and you will be safe and secure in God's everlasting arms.

Forgiving yourself, as we will see in more detail later, is something you must keep on doing. In *Total Forgiveness* I call it a "life sentence." Like some medicines, which one has to take as long as one lives, so is forgiving those who have hurt you something you do forever—unless it is not an issue anymore. But whenever the devil reminds you of what "they" have done, and it brings you down, then you forgive them all over again. So too with totally forgiving ourselves. We may go for a good while, not feeling any sense of shame for our past failures and shortcomings, but should the devil bring something to your attention, with the express purpose of causing you to lose your joy and freedom, simply forgive yourself all over again. That is what we all have to do.

One last thing. The devil knows that "his time is short" (Rev. 12:12). He knows his final destiny (Matt. 8:29; Rev. 20:10). The next time the devil reminds you of your past, you remind him of his future.

PART III

How to Forgive
Ourselves

CHAPTER 7

SPIRITUAL GIANTS

The best of men are men at best.

—ANONYMOUS

Misery loves company.

—ENGLISH PROVERB

But we have this treasure in jars of clay to show that this all-surpassing power is from God and not from us.... For our light and momentary troubles are achieving for us an eternal glory that far outweighs them all.

—2 CORINTHIANS 4:7, 17

It gives me no small comfort to know that those people God used most had a lot to answer for. If God can love and use people like Jacob or King David, which He did, then He can surely love and use you and me. I find this very encouraging. For one thing, these two men were possibly the worst parents described in the Old Testament.

It may come as no great surprise to you that many biblical giants had skeletons in their cupboards. Except that their skeletons did not remain there! The biblical writers told it all—unlike most biographies about people in recent centuries in which you seldom read very much that would embarrass them if they were alive. We want our heroes on pedestals! Biographers, not to mention those who write autobiographies, are pretty careful not to make the person look *too* bad! But Holy Scripture does not omit or gloss over the defects of its heroes. You can read for yourself! In any case, we will examine some of them and see how they managed to live with themselves after they made such horrid mistakes. Some of these giants had awful memories to cope with.

I am not sure if the concept of forgiving oneself was consciously uppermost in the minds of those who lived in biblical times. This kind of language might have come around more recently. But one thing is for sure: human nature has not changed one bit in four thousand years, and, what is equally important to remember, they, like us, had consciences; they all had to live with themselves. You may be sure some of them felt guilt and shame for their ethical and moral failures. One of the reasons I have waited a good while to write this present book after *Total Forgiveness* was that I needed to be sure how to treat some of these people and see whether they had a problem with forgiving themselves and whether they did it. Follow me, therefore, in this survey of some of God's best-known servants.

JACOB

Also known as Israel, Jacob is the best example I can think of that shows the *sheer grace of God.* He is one nonstop illustration from birth to burial of how God continues to love, overrule, and look after a selfish, manipulative, insensitive, and complaining man. God never stopped loving Jacob and never ceased blessing him, although it must be said that Jacob knew a lot of suffering as well.

Why is this important for you and me? If you are like me, you agree with the old English proverb, "Misery loves company." I sometimes think that my own failure must embarrass the angels and that I must be the worst example of a Christian leader of all time! Forgive me, but that is the truth. But when I see how much God looked after Jacob, I tell myself that God loves to specialize in difficult cases! That gives me hope.

And I trust it gives you hope. Not that all that was true of Jacob would be true of you; neither would all that is true of you or me characterize those in the Bible we will look at. But we are all susceptible to the most regrettable sins, and, apart from the grace of God, we could commit any sin or crime ever recorded in human history. As the saying goes, "There, but for the grace of God, go I."

Jacob's mother, Rebekah, knew that she had twins in her womb (Esau and Jacob) and that God chose Jacob over Esau (Gen. 25:21–23; Mal. 1:2–3; Rom. 9:13). She was no doubt governed by this and probably had no small hand in teaching Jacob some of his manipulative ways. If indeed every person is worth understanding, you should know that Jacob was a mama's boy and grew up without ever bonding with his father, Isaac. Let me summarize the life of Jacob as follows.

Jacob as a brother to Esau

The first thing Jacob did was to take unfair advantage of Esau's hunger and tiredness and persuade his weakened brother to sell his birthright before he was fed and refreshed. Once Esau gave in, it was too late for him to change it (Gen. 25:29–34; Heb. 12:16–17). This was a cruel thing for Jacob to do to his brother.

Some time later, through the coaxing of Rebekah, Jacob repeated his trickery in order to get Isaac's patriarchal blessing (Gen. 27:1–29). It worked, but Jacob spent the rest of his life in perpetual, nagging fear that Esau would eventually find him and kill him (Gen. 27:41).

But there is more. Years later, when Esau sent word that he was indeed coming to see Jacob, this, predictably, sent tremors through Jacob's soul. He was so afraid that he did not even join the rest of his family at first, but that was also the occasion when he wrestled with God and was given the name Israel (Gen. 32:22–38). The meeting with Esau turned out to be surprisingly friendly—to Jacob's utter relief (Gen. 33:1–11). But Jacob still did not trust Esau, always fearing the worst. Consequently he refused Esau's invitation that they spend more time together (Gen. 33:12–17).

In a word: Jacob had no positive relationship with his brother whatsoever.

Jacob as a son to his father, Isaac

Jacob could not help it that he was not close to his father. He was no doubt influenced by Rebekah, who clearly preferred Jacob over Esau. What is more, Isaac clearly preferred Esau because of Esau's love of the open country and ability to cook wild game (Gen. 25:28). But no small ingredient in the relationship was that Esau was the firstborn and stood to inherit the greater blessing one day.

But in the end Jacob showed himself to be a rogue by his deceitful manipulation of his own father to get Isaac's patriarchal blessing instead of it coming to Esau.

Pretending to be Esau, Jacob approached and took advantage of his blind father, then succeeded in securing the coveted, valuable, and irrevocable blessing of Isaac (Gen. 27:27–29). This too was an awful thing to do, but as I said, Jacob paid for it with deep, deep dread and fear the rest of his life.

Jacob as a husband

Jacob fell in love with Rachel, the daughter of Laban—a relative for whom Jacob agreed to work for a while. Laban promised Jacob that he could marry Rachel in exchange for seven years of employment. But on the morning after the wedding, strange as it may seem, it was not Rachel Jacob slept with but Leah, Rachel's less attractive sister. Laban had manipulated Jacob! Angry that this should happen, Jacob nonetheless agreed to work another seven years for Laban in order to get Rachel.

Leah, a prime example of an unloved wife, possibly did more for the future kingdom of God than Jacob's beloved Rachel did. Leah gave Jacob six sons, among them Levi (whose legacy was the Levitical priesthood) and Judah (through whom the Messiah came). When Leah gave birth to Jacob's firstborn, Reuben, she said, "Surely my husband will love me now" (Gen. 29:32). When she was pregnant with Levi, she expressed the wish, "Now at last my husband will become attached to me" (Gen. 29:34), but he never did. Jacob never appreciated Leah.

Although Jacob loved Rachel, he was hardly the perfect husband to her. Not caring how deeply she felt that she could not have children, Jacob became annoyed and rebuked her, "Am I in the place of God, who has kept you from having children?" (Gen. 30:2). But Rachel eventually gave birth to two sons: Joseph and Benjamin.

Jacob as a father to Dinah

The first indication of the kind of father Jacob would turn out to be was evidenced when his sons rescued his daughter, Dinah, from the Shechemites. Instead of showing gratitude to his sons for what they did, he said to Simeon and Levi, "You have brought trouble on me by making me a stench to the Canaanites and Perizzites"

(Gen. 34:30). He wasn't even proud of his sons for what they did. He cared little for Dinah herself, only thinking of himself.

Jacob as a father to Joseph

Like father, like son. As Isaac showed favoritism, loving Esau more than Jacob, Jacob showed favoritism, preferring Joseph over the other sons (Gen. 37:3). When a parent shows partiality like this, they do no child a favor, whether to the one who gets the special attention (Jacob gave Joseph a richly ornamented robe, traditionally called the "coat of many colors") or the other siblings who feel rejected by the parent. Showing favoritism like that puts every son or daughter in a no-win situation. Furthermore, it was Jacob's partiality to Joseph that even led to the brothers' betrayal of Joseph and their selling him to the Ishmaelites (Gen. 37:4–28). The irony is, in his preference for Joseph, he ended up losing Joseph for a long time and thus divided his family for years and years. This was a dysfunctional family if there ever was one. Jacob had a lot to answer for.

Jacob as a father to the other sons

After the brothers wickedly sold Joseph to the Ishmaelites, you will recall that they took Joseph's robe off him, dipped it in blood, and laid it before old Jacob, who took the bait. "Some ferocious animal has devoured him," he said. Although his family came to comfort him, he "refused to be comforted" but said, "in mourning will I go down to the grave to my son" (Gen. 37:33–35).

Some time later, after the sons of Jacob returned from Egypt, where they went to buy food, they reported that the prime minister required that they leave Simeon behind in Egypt until they brought Benjamin.

What follows is not Jacob's finest hour. First, he blamed his sons for all the bad things that had happened to him: "*You* have deprived me of my children…and now you want to take Benjamin. Everything is against me!" (Gen. 42:36, emphasis added). But there was more. After stating that Benjamin would not go to Egypt with the sons, he then dealt the severest blow and most hurtful insult to them that you can imagine: he said to his own flesh and blood that Benjamin "is the only one left." Think about that! How would you like it if your father looked at you and said that your brother is his only living son? Jacob did not even regard the rest of his sons as his own! What rejection they must have felt!

Jacob and the fruit of the Holy Spirit

This may be unfair, but I have to say that I am amazed that this historic, patriarchal figure could be so apparently devoid of what today we would call the fruit of the Spirit, such as "love, joy, peace, patience, kindness, goodness, faithfulness, gentleness and self-control" (Gal. 5:22). If anybody should make Jacob their hero, I shudder to think what kind of leader or person he or she would be! Jacob was a self-centered, controlling, and uncaring man. And yet I suspect there are leaders like that today. There are also mentors around who will not admit to a mistake, never show their "clay feet," or never acknowledge a specific weakness. You may have heard of the philosophy "never explain, never complain, never apologize." This was Jacob to a degree—but he was a complainer!

Did Jacob ever forgive himself? If so, how?

First, it is impossible for us to get into Jacob's mind to that extent. We don't know for sure whether he ever felt truly ashamed of himself. He must have! He must have felt enormous guilt! But he doesn't reveal it. We don't know if he even felt the need to forgive himself. There is a type of person—sometimes a leader, sometimes a parent—who feels they must show unwavering strength, power, and authority; that it would diminish their self-respect, sense of dignity, and honor to manifest the slightest vulnerability. Jacob was apparently like that. All we know for sure is he truly felt *grief.* But I don't know if he felt *guilt.*

So what if he didn't? What if he never even felt the need to ask forgiveness from God or to forgive himself? He certainly did not feel a need to ask his sons or his unloved Leah to forgive him; much less did he manifest a sense of shame over his dictatorial and ungrateful ways. So what if he felt no need for *any* kind of forgiveness?

I reply: God was infinitely—even if it seems unfair—gracious to Jacob: "Jacob I loved" (Rom. 9:13). I have concluded that the Lord so overruled Jacob's obvious infirmities that He not only guided him continually but also overwhelmed him with grace when he needed it. Jacob very possibly took such grace as God's approval without any further need to admit to any fault or poor judgment. I don't know whether the idea of "sense of sin" as I have expounded in this book was a patriarchal characteristic, but, as I said, we cannot get that deeply into his mind. On the one hand I want to say that he *must* have felt ashamed of himself. But what if he wasn't?

Like it or not, it would seem that, sadly, Jacob was simply not self-conscious of his deeply flawed character—and yet God still blessed him anyway. Yes, Jacob went through the whole of his life blaming everybody but himself, feeling sorry for himself, and yet apparently unconscious of a sense of sin or shame. If this is indeed true, he would have felt no need to apply Robert Burns's famous lines:

> O wad some Pow'r the giftie gie us
> To see oursels as others see us.[1]

It seems to me, therefore, that Jacob never saw himself as we see him, neither can we prove that he would have cared all that much if he did!

I therefore wonder if God chose to let Jacob be an example of sheer grace if only to demonstrate how much God can love unworthy people: "What *if* he did this to make the riches of his glory known to the objects of his mercy, whom he prepared in advance for glory?" (Rom. 9:23, emphasis added). After all, God said to Moses, "I will have mercy on whom I have mercy, and I will have compassion on whom I have compassion" (Rom. 9:15).

What I also know is this: God intervened time after time in Jacob's life, encouraged him to move to Egypt (Gen. 46:3), and restored his relationship to Joseph (Gen. 46:29), bestowing on him blessing after blessing and grace upon grace. The only thing that the "faith chapter" of the Bible says about this unworthy man is that Jacob, or Israel, whose name occurs more times than any other in the Old Testament, "when he was dying, blessed each of Joseph's sons, and worshiped as he leaned on the top of his staff" (Heb. 11:21). This is why I gave as a title of my book on Jacob *All's Well That Ends Well.*

Here is my conclusion: God simply overwhelmed Jacob with such exceeding tenderness and love that Jacob probably never gave the idea of forgiving himself much thought, if any.

You may ask, "Then why use Jacob as an example? How can we learn from him as to how to forgive ourselves?"

I reply: I refer to him for two reasons. First, there are those, perhaps not unlike Jacob even today, who are not bothered about things such as asking for forgiveness or having to forgive oneself. You and I may feel indignant that such people don't worry about this. I have had to watch myself and not judge when I see what seems to me to be utterly unjust—by people who should know better! But no doubt there are those who have thought the same of me, too. In any case, don't be surprised if people do things and apparently feel no sense of guilt. There are people like that, and you and I should not be judgmental of them! If they don't perceive that they need to ask forgiveness or forgive themselves, let's not point the finger at *them* but rather take people as they are and not try to squeeze them into our mold.

Secondly, the main reason I have chosen to reference Jacob in this book is that his example should encourage anybody. You can read the entire life of Jacob (from Genesis 25:21 to Genesis 50:26) and see for yourself that God kept loving him despite his shortcomings. That is, to my way of thinking, a very strong hint from God that we can borrow from this story and apply it fully to ourselves. It is my view that there is a little Jacob in all of us. When I know that God loved, used, and (undoubtedly) *forgave* Jacob for his sins, I can say to myself, "God can love me, too!" and also say, "I should not *struggle* over having to forgive myself after knowing how God loved, used, and forgave Jacob." In other words, I find it much, much easier to forgive myself by knowing what I do about Jacob. And that is mainly why I have referred to him: to inspire and encourage you to put your past behind you. After all, if everything that was so extraordinarily complicated and wrong in the life of Jacob could work together for good—and it certainly did (Rom. 8:28)—you too will be able to say that *all's well that ends well.*

DAVID

The only person in the Bible described as a man after God's own heart (1 Sam. 13:14; Acts 13:22), King David was an example of the grace of God as Jacob was—with this difference: Moses, who wrote Genesis, does not allow us to get very deeply into Jacob's conscious feelings, but the writer of the life of David lets us see how David felt. Besides that, we have David's own feelings displayed in many of his psalms.

David's greed, lust, and murder

David had several wives and many concubines. God gave him the house of Judah and Israel, and if that were not enough, He said to David, "I would have given you even more" (2 Sam. 12:8). But all this apparently did not satisfy David. One day David saw a beautiful woman bathing. David's lust seized him. Inquiring who she was, he was told that her name was Bathsheba and that she was married to Uriah, one of David's soldiers. That should have stopped him. It didn't. He invited her to his palace and slept with her. What might have been a one-off afternoon affair became complicated when she sent word to David a few weeks later that she was pregnant. Then David conceived the idea of bringing Uriah home for the weekend to sleep with his wife. But as we saw earlier, Uriah had an "overly scrupulous conscience," and he refused to sleep with Bathsheba. David therefore ordered Uriah to be stationed in the hottest part of the battle. It worked. Uriah was killed (2 Sam. 11).

David loved Bathsheba and brought her as his wife to his house, and she gave birth to a son. There follows the writer's comment that all men and women should read again and again: "But the thing David had done displeased the LORD" (2 Sam. 11:27). When we do what has displeased God, we should *repent at once* or prepare for Him to step in. If He doesn't, it is a bad sign—that we won't even be chastened since He only disciplines those He loves (Heb. 12:6). Those who are dealt with for their folly in this life are in fact blessed. "Why should any *living* man complain when punished for his sins?" (Lam. 3:39, emphasis added). While we are still alive and judged, it is very good news indeed; it means we will not be condemned with the world, which would mean being eternally lost

(1 Cor. 11:32). To put it another way, if God never disciplines you, it is ominous that He lets you get away with stuff that is wrong. Bad sign. God does not discipline those who are not His own.

But God sent the prophet Nathan to show David that, although he thought he had gotten away with his sin, a grieved heavenly Father now decided to step in. It was approximately *two years* after the sin was committed that Nathan came to him. David knew full well he had displeased God but somehow thought his sin would be overlooked. What is interesting but sad is that there was no sign of sorrow or repentance during these two years. In other words, had not Nathan come to him, David might have gone on indefinitely without repentance!

It is interesting to me that David apparently felt no guilt at first for his adultery and murder, but was "conscience-stricken after he had counted the fighting men." He said to the Lord, "I have sinned greatly in what I have done. Now, O Lord, I beg you, take away the guilt of your servant. I have done a very foolish thing" (2 Sam. 24:10). Why he felt this for numbering the people and not for his adultery and murder is beyond me, unless he had developed a better sense of sin by this time, which I choose to believe. With the adultery and murder, God sent the prophet Nathan two years after; with counting the sin of the people, David felt convicted before the prophet Gad came to him.

If someone lovingly comes to *you* if you have been "caught in a sin" (Gal. 6:1), you should not resent them but fall to your knees and thank God that He cares so much for you so as to caution you and restore you.

But David did not get off with a mere caution from Nathan. First, Nathan began his speech before the king with a kind of parable, describing a rich man who took advantage of a poor man who had nothing except one little ewe lamb, whereupon the rich man took the ewe lamb away from the poor man. David burned with anger and said to Nathan, "As surely as the LORD lives, the man who did this deserves to die!" Then Nathan said to David, "You are the man!" God had revealed to Nathan exactly what David had done: sleeping with Bathsheba, murdering Uriah, and taking Bathsheba as his wife.

There was good news and bad news from Nathan to David. The good news: God would forgive the sin and not take David's life. According to the Law, David's sin should be punished by being stoned to death. But Nathan said to David, "You are not going to die." The bad news was that "the sword will never depart from your house." Moreover, the "son born to you will die," said Nathan (2 Sam. 12:1–15).

David was not defensive. On the spot he said, "I have sinned against the LORD" (2 Sam. 12:13). Had he been defensive or dismissive of Nathan, David would have been in deeper trouble. The worst thing we can do when God rolls up His sleeve to judge us is to argue back with Him or deny what we have done. We should take His gracious judgment with both hands. David, the man after God's own heart, did this. He was truly sorry. Psalm 51, to which we will return below, is David's prayer of confession and repentance.

David as a father to his children

The first overt hint of God's judgment upon the house of King David was when his son Amnon fell in love with his sister, Tamar. David was so detached from his family that he saw nothing odd about Amnon's strange request to the king. Pretending to be ill, Amnon asked the king to request Tamar to come to his quarters and "make some special bread in my sight, so I may eat from her hand." David asked no questions but sent word to Tamar: "Go to the house of your brother Amnon and prepare some food for him."

But when she came to Amnon, he grabbed her, asking her to come to bed with him, and then raped her (2 Sam. 13:1–14).

Tamar shared this tragic news with Absalom, her other brother. Absalom did nothing for two years, but one day, unexpectedly, Absalom got revenge upon Amnon and killed him. Absalom fled to another country where he stayed three years. David mourned the loss of his son Amnon in the meantime. He knew that all this was but the unfolding of Nathan's prophecy, "the sword will never depart from your house." After three years Absalom returned to Jerusalem, and the relationship between Absalom and David was restored (2 Sam. 14).

But if only that were the end of the story. Once Absalom was in Jerusalem, he managed steal "the hearts of the men of Israel." The eventual result was that King David had to flee from Jerusalem. It is one of the most melancholy episodes in all Holy Writ. David took all this with dignity, knowing full well that it was still a part of Nathan's prophecy. When Zadok the priest wanted to bring the ark of God with David in his exile, the king said to Zadok, "Take the ark of God back into the city. If I find favor in the LORD's eyes, he will bring me back and let me see it and his dwelling place again. But if he says, 'I am not pleased with you,' then I am ready; let him do to me whatever seems good to him" (2 Sam. 15:25–26). During this time one called Shimei cursed the king as he fled. He pelted David with stones. When Abishai wanted to defend David, the king replied, "Leave him alone; let him curse, for the LORD has told him to. It may be that the LORD will see my distress and repay me with good for the cursing I am receiving today" (2 Sam. 16:11–12). This is the model example of how you and I should respond to God's chastening, should this happen to us.

And yet there is more. Absalom himself was judged and was killed in the battle in which he hoped to kill his own father. David wept for Absalom, crying, "If only I had died instead of you—O Absalom, my son, my son!" (2 Sam. 18:33). But, as we saw earlier, David went too far in his mourning. It became self-pity; he nearly lost his own following. But his close friend Joab firmly warned David to snap out of it and show himself in regal authority (2 Sam. 19:1–8).

David's prayer in Psalm 51 shows his profound sorrow, confession of his sin, and repentance. There is every reason to believe that David also forgave himself as well. There was no beating himself black and blue. He confessed his sin, asked for the cleansing of the blood, prayed for joy and gladness, and affirmed, "Then I will teach transgressors your ways, and sinners will turn back to you" (Ps. 51:13). The best proof, however, that he forgave himself was in these words: "The sacrifices of God are a broken spirit; a broken and contrite heart, O God, you will not despise"—which David knew perfectly described him (Ps. 51:17). David took his forgiveness from God with open arms and never looked back.

Finally, what are called "the last words of David" show a man at total peace with himself: "Is not my house right with God? Has he not made with me an everlasting covenant, arranged and secured in every part? Will he not bring to fruition my salvation and grant me my every desire?" (2 Sam. 23:5).

Unlike Jacob, then, who admitted to no guilt for anything, only revealing self-pity, David comes through as a trophy of grace, forgiveness, and acceptance of himself.

SIMON PETER

I think many of us identify quite a bit with Peter, not because he was the most colorful of the twelve disciples of Jesus, but because he was so prone to say the wrong thing at the wrong time so much of the time. Also, he honestly thought that he was the most devoted of the Twelve and was shocked that Jesus would say to him, "Before the rooster crows, you will disown me three times!" (John 13:38). Jesus said this to him immediately after Peter said, "I will lay down my life for you" (v. 37).

That should teach us all a lesson. When we are feeling close to God and in a bit of a pious mood, perhaps we should be guarded in boasting how much we love Him. He knows us backward and forward, and I would hate to think what He might say to me were I to speak too confidently to Him of my ardent loyalty.

As the Lord had prophesied, within hours Peter denied knowing Jesus to a Galilean servant girl. When the rooster crowed, Peter remembered the word of Jesus, and "he went outside and wept bitterly" (Matt. 26:75).

It is good to know that our failings do not take God by surprise. He not only understands us through and through, but He also knows the end from the beginning. Jesus even said to Peter, "Simon, Simon, Satan has asked to sift you as wheat. But I have prayed for you, Simon, that your faith may not fail. And when you have turned back ["converted," KJV], strengthen your brothers" (Luke 22:31–32). It is also noteworthy that in John's gospel, Jesus's prophecy of Peter's denial was followed with these famous words, directed to all of the disciples: "Do not let your hearts be troubled. Trust in God; trust also in me" (John 14:1). In other words, it was as though our Lord said, "I know what is coming. I know you will deny Me. I also know that all of you will forsake Me and flee, but do not be troubled. You do believe in God; believe in Me." That is the way we are loved with an everlasting love.

After His resurrection from the dead, Jesus appeared in a room behind locked doors where ten of the disciples had gathered and were fearful and feeling very, very guilty. Jesus had a word for them that must have overwhelmed them: "Peace be with you! As the Father has sent me, I am sending you" (John 20:21). What? After all that happened? No moralizing, no shaming them, no making them feel guilty? Not a word. Just "peace be with you." It was as though nothing had happened! Jesus merely picked up where He had left off!

And who was the preacher on the Day of Pentecost, preaching the inaugural sermon of the church? Simon Peter. He was a forgiven man. Furthermore, had he not *felt* forgiven, he would not have been able to stand boldly before thousands of Jews as he did! The anointing of the Spirit comes on a person like that who is not only forgiven but who has also forgiven himself or herself.

You will say, "But Jesus made it easy for them." Yes, He certainly did. And He does precisely the same thing with you. Instead of adding salt to your wounds, rubbing your nose in your shame, and making you "pay" with greater guilt for your failure, He says to you, "As the Father sent me, so I send you. Strengthen your brothers and sisters. Teach transgressors my ways."

PAUL

The skeletons in Paul's cupboard were all in his pre-Christian past. Perhaps it is easier for some to forgive themselves for what they did prior to their coming to Christ. Many people who have written me or who used to come to see me at Westminster Chapel worried more about what they have done or let happen *since* they were saved. I can easily identify with people like this. I was only six years old when I was converted. So what I have to forgive myself for is all in my postconversion past! However, Paul did such terrible things before he was converted that some have opined (though I don't agree) that his "thorn in the flesh" was the guilt he felt over what he did to Christians before he was saved.

The truth is, perhaps not unlike Moses, Paul had a lot to answer for. Moses, who would later give us the Ten Commandments that included the injunction "You shall not murder" (Exod. 20:13), had himself committed murder. One day Moses observed an Egyptian beating a Hebrew. "Glancing this way and that and seeing no one, he killed the Egyptian and hid him in the sand." But he found out soon that act had "become known." Pharaoh heard about it and tried to kill Moses. It is what caused him to flee from Pharaoh forever (Exod. 2:12–15). To explain how Moses coped with this would be to enter into unprofitable speculation.

Luke tells us what Paul did before he was saved. Having approved of the Jews' stoning Stephen (Acts 8:1), "Saul [as he was first known] began to destroy the church. Going from house to house, he dragged off men and women and put them in prison" (Acts 8:3). Years after his extraordinary conversion, Paul testified to King Agrippa:

> On the authority of the chief priests I put many of the saints in prison, and when they were put to death, I cast my vote against them. Many a time I went from one synagogue to another to have them punished, and I tried to force them to blaspheme. In my obsession against them, I even went to foreign cities to persecute them.
>
> —ACTS 26:10–11

I think it is reasonable to suppose that Paul not only accepted God's total forgiveness of these horrible sins but also forgave himself the moment he felt God's forgiveness. The Lord Jesus appeared to Saul on the road to Damascus and said to him, "Saul, Saul, why do you persecute me?" (Acts 9:4). Paul was instantly converted. He was told by the Lord what to do, and he obeyed. He was also given a mandate to preach, mainly to the Gentiles, and preach to them "forgiveness of sins" (Acts 26:15–18).

It will do no good to speculate as to how deeply shameful Paul felt about what he did. I only know he referred to what he did when he wrote the Philippians (Phil. 3:6), then said, "One thing I do: *Forgetting what is behind* and straining toward what is ahead, I press on toward the goal to win the prize for which God has called me heavenward in Christ Jesus" (Phil. 3:13–14, emphasis added).

Some of us who have difficulty forgiving ourselves may resent those who so easily forgive themselves. Corrie ten Boom tells of her seeing the very man who had been so cruel to her beloved sister in prison sitting in the church service to hear Corrie speak. Corrie had to pray for special grace. That is not all; after the service he came to her and said how good God was to forgive all our sins. But Corrie fought further resentment that he could accept God's forgiveness so readily and speak to her without any great sense of guilt and shame. The truth is, she could not know what this man may have secretly suffered over the years, just as we don't know what sense of guilt and shame Jacob felt.

I only know that you and I are utter fools if we do not take God's total forgiveness with both hands and greater fools if we refuse to forgive ourselves totally and opt instead to dwell on the past. If God could use a Jacob, a Moses, a David, a Peter, and a Saul of Tarsus—all of whom had so much to answer for—God can use you and me. He has made it as clear as He possibly can that you are to forgive yourself *totally* and not look at what is behind.

There is one more episode in Paul's life that I find incredible. It is one of the best examples in the Bible I have come across that shows absolutely *no guilt* when one might think Paul should have felt very guilty indeed. It is when he went to Troas to preach. He also expected to meet Titus there. He admits in his letter to the Corinthians that he "had no peace of mind" that Titus was not in Troas where Paul had gone for the stated purpose "to preach the gospel of Christ." And thus it turns out that Paul had a more urgent reason for going to Troas—to meet up with Titus. But Titus wasn't there. Paul was so upset that Titus was not there that he walked away from an open door and went to Macedonia instead to look for Titus!

This to me is extraordinary. Imagine it: the great apostle Paul, who admits that "the Lord had opened a door for me" in Troas to preach the gospel of Christ, was so preoccupied with needing to see Titus that he left! "I said good-by to them and went on to Macedonia." And to think that he admitted this in writing to the Corinthians! (See 2 Corinthians 2:12–13.) He left himself extremely open to the most vehement criticism by his opponents (of which there were many) that he would put a personal concern before his calling to preach. But that is exactly what he tells us! This shows me one more thing about Paul (I wish I were more like this): he was so devoid of any kind of guilt—pseudoguilt or true guilt—that he was not afraid to make himself so vulnerable. As my friend Pete Cantrell loves to say, "The greatest freedom is having nothing to prove."

Paul had such a freedom. This to me is a breathtaking example of having totally forgiven oneself. Most of all, he wasn't the slightest bit worried about what God might think! He then explained why; he had a sweet security in his relationship to Christ, not to mention a robust theology of the sovereignty of God:

> But thanks be to God, who always leads us in triumphal procession in Christ and through us spreads everywhere the fragrance of the knowledge of him. For we are to God the aroma of Christ among those who are being saved and those who are perishing. To the one we are the smell of death; to the other, the fragrance of life.
>
> —2 CORINTHIANS 2:14–16

CHAPTER 8

ACCEPTING OURSELVES

Don't cherish exaggerated ideas of yourself or your importance, but try to have a sane estimate of your capabilities by the light of the faith that God has given to you all.

—ROMANS 12:3–4, PHILLIPS

By the grace of God I am what I am.

—1 CORINTHIANS 15:10

You were made by God and for God—and until you understand that, life will never make sense.

—RICK WARREN[1]

Perhaps you are like someone who said to me recently, "My problem is not in forgiving myself but *accepting* myself."

Accepting yourself means that you have positively come to terms with the way God has made you and shaped you. It is perhaps better defined as the *absence of the negative,* that is, when you no longer reject yourself and are no longer in denial or are hostile to the way you are. God wants this for you. It is what pleases Him *so much;* after all (if you will receive this), you are the product of His own dealings with you. Not that you have "arrived" or anything like that, but that you see yourself as a work in progress—a work of which your heavenly Father is at the bottom.

Take Christmas, for example. As I write these words, it happens to be Christmastime. The joy of Christmas for me is not receiving a present but giving it and watching the looks on the face of my wife, our son and daughter-in-law, our daughter, and other friends when they open their presents. When I see them so happy, it makes me so happy!

In this way, then, God is *so happy* when you accept yourself. It is accepting His gift to you, namely, the thought and care and time that He has put in over the years in order to bring you to where you are at this moment. He is waiting for you to accept His gift, which in this case is *you as you now are.*

If, however, you are not happy with the way you now are, then consider that God isn't finished with you yet and, just maybe, a year from now (hopefully sooner) you will say to God, "Thank You for the time and care that has gone into shaping me and bringing me to accept myself as I am."

There is something you can do that nobody else can do as well. The reason that nobody else can do it as well is because they are not like you. If you were different, you could not do what you are now qualified to do; for example, sympathize with others, encourage others, and bless others.

God has been shaping your life for many years to bring you to where you are so that you can be His instrument to your generation.

Until you can truly accept yourself, however, you will be limited in the way you can bless others. The reason for this is that you will lack the self-confidence and self-esteem that are required in order to pass maximum blessing on to others.

I can remember the early days when I stood at the steps of Westminster Chapel in Buckingham Gate on Saturday mornings giving out Christian pamphlets. I was nervous and fearful. The more people would reject my tracts and say unkind words, the more uneasy I felt. But there came a day I decided to...yes, smile. I forced it. I didn't feel like smiling—believe me. But I did it anyway. I learned something immediately. Whereas one out of ten were accepting a leaflet when I did not smile, *over half* of the people who came along began accepting my literature. Why? It showed in my face. I came to terms that if God wanted me to be a pilot light in the streets of Victoria, I should affirm *Him* by looking happy about it! It worked. It was never the same again.

When we are unhappy with the way God made us, where He has put us, and what He has called us to do, we will be chronically ineffective. It is as simple as that. But when we are happy with the way God made us and shaped us, we become His instruments of peace and joy.

By the way, by forcing a smile I began eventually to *feel* like smiling. And my whole perspective changed, not to mention the results: people stopping to talk, some of whom prayed the sinner's prayer in front of the Chapel.

As Satan does not want you to forgive yourself and will accuse you and bring up your past, so too does Satan not want you to accept yourself. He wants you to hate yourself. Forgive me, but if you hate yourself, you are at the moment a part of Satan's success with you. Don't give him that satisfaction! Satan is behind your negative thoughts. We are God's creation, and Satan hates what God has created.

The Holy Spirit will give you positive thoughts about yourself. What comes from the Holy Spirit is the polar opposite to thoughts from the devil. Learn to recognize, refuse, and resist those negative thoughts about yourself.

Creation + Environment + the Holy Spirit = the Way God Has Made You

When I speak of the way God has made you, I do not mean merely His choice of your parents or what you were like when you were born. That is only a part of the way God has made you. You will recall the illustration that we are all tips of an iceberg, 90 percent of us being submerged in the sea, 10 percent being what people see. What is therefore submerged in the sea—your parental care (or lack of it), your early memories (many forgotten) of childhood, your peers, your teachers, your mentors, your heroes, your enemies, and even your casual acquaintances—is a part of the way God has made you. Because the way you have been shaped is the way God chose to make you. It is all a part of forming you into the person you now are.

Therefore you must accept that your birth and all that has happened to you since is a part of the way God has determined to make you. But that is not all; you are a new creation in Christ Jesus (2 Cor. 5:17). The consequence is that you are a new person. All that God did at the natural level—creation—is augmented by what He has been doing at the supernatural level by the Holy Spirit. The result: you are His "workmanship," "God's work of art" (JB), "God's handiwork" (NEB), and "what we are" (PHILLIPS) because of the Holy Spirit (Eph. 2:10).

You are no accident. "My parents did not want me," you may reply to me. I believe you. *But God wanted you.* You were known from the foundation of the world, before the beginning of time (2 Tim. 1:9). God not only "determined" the time when you were born and the "times set for them"—meaning the cultural, social, political, and environmental situation of the particular generation in which you were born—but He also determined "the exact places" where each person born should live (Acts 17:26).

Here is the goal God has envisaged for you: that you will agree with all He has said about you, namely, that God created your "inmost being" and you were knit together in your mother's womb (Ps. 139:13). God did that. Not you. Not your parents. God. If it has not crossed your mind to speak like this yet, I pray that you will one day say with the psalmist:

> I praise you because I am fearfully and wonderfully made; your works are wonderful, I know that full well. My frame was not hidden from you when I was made in the secret place. When I was woven together in the depths of the earth, your eyes saw my unformed body. All the days ordained for me were written in your book before one of them came to be. How precious to me are your thoughts, O God! How vast is the sum of them! Were I to count them, they would outnumber the grains of sand.
>
> —PSALM 139:14–18

The next time you should see a grain of sand, remember these lines. God's thoughts about you outnumber the grains of sand in this world. That means a lot of thoughts! God chose you as though there were nobody else, and, as St. Augustine put it a long time ago, "He loves every person as if there were no one else to love." It pleases Him so much when we accept ourselves like this. That is what He wants for you, and that is the reason for this chapter.

WHAT ACCEPTING YOURSELF IS NOT

It does not mean accepting that you are a finished product as you now are.

Accepting yourself does not mean that you have "arrived" and do not need any improvement. You are not to see yourself as being "as good as it gets." You and I are en route to the next level of grace and glory that God has in mind for us. As I said, we are a work in progress. The apostle Paul had great goals for himself, including knowing Christ and the power of His resurrection *and* becoming utterly like Jesus. He immediately admitted that the fulfillment of this desire was still in the future. He said he had not "already obtained" this, not yet "succeeded" (GNB), or "achieved" (PHILLIPS) this lofty goal. Nor will you in this life. But you should also say with Paul, "One thing I do: Forgetting what is behind and straining toward what is ahead, I press on toward the goal to win the prize for which God has called me heavenward in Christ Jesus" (Phil. 3:10–14).

It does not mean accepting your continued sinning.

This is extremely important. If you have weaknesses and temptations that you fully intend—deliberately, willfully, and consciously—to give in to today and tomorrow, you are not accepting yourself in a God-honoring manner. This would be to abuse the very teaching of this chapter. I don't say I don't sympathize with your temptation or weakness (which I will deal with below); I must lovingly tell you that to give in to and plan to keep giving in to continued sin is to play into Satan's plan for your life. You will not be able to live with yourself, or, to put it mildly, you will live in complete denial and could end up with a seared conscience (1 Tim. 4:2). Please don't be a fool. When you repeatedly give in to temptation so that it becomes a sin but say, "I accept myself," it is the opposite of what I am teaching now.

It is not accepting your present spiritual progress as final.

The truth is, we all need more grace. The truth is, none of us are perfect. The truth is, I need to be better than I am. I will share with you a rather embarrassing discovery on my part: every time I have begun to feel that I have at long last "got the victory" over a particular fault or malady in my life, I soon fall flat on my face! When I am enjoying a time of victory over this or that weakness, I have learned not to jump the gun but say, "Whoa!" Why? Because it is only a matter of time until I will find myself repeating an old sin that I thought I was over and done with. It is one thing to plan to sin, but quite another to fall into it when you had planned otherwise. But we will always be sinners to some degree (1 John 1:8–10).

It is not accepting your present knowledge as final.

Some people do not want to learn. They "know it all" already and don't want to be bothered with a contrary point of view. This could refer to theological knowledge, knowledge concerning your job or things you are generally good at, or any knowledge that could make you wiser, stronger, and broader in your perspective. There are three possibilities:

1. Ever learning but never able to come to the knowledge of the truth (2 Tim. 3:7)

2. Learning all the time but also coming into knowledge of the truth, which sets you free (2 Cor. 3:17–18)

3. Never wanting to learn because you are content with your present status of knowledge

Some people are threatened by a different point of view or new information that would expose their need for more knowledge. Don't you be like that!

It is not accepting your present situation as final.
This could refer to a number of things, some of which I will deal with below. In a word: do not hastily presume that your present situation, your job, your calling, your friends, your location, your hobbies, or your interests are all there is. It could be that God has new things for you that you could not have conceived of (1 Cor. 2:9). Behold, God told Isaiah, "I am doing a new thing!" (Isa. 43:19). The truth is, God isn't finished with you yet and has much more in mind for you than you have thought! Don't let the devil have a victory over you by telling you, "What you now have is as good as it will get." Remember: Satan is a liar.

What Accepting Yourself Is

Before I get into the particulars, I must say that accepting and *approving* are not necessarily the same thing. Accepting and *being thrilled* with something is not necessarily the same thing. The first distinction may be delicate and subtle, but approval essentially means to have a favorable opinion of something. I am not asking that you have a favorable opinion of what I will deal with below, and I am certainly not suggesting that you be thrilled with these things. Who can ask anybody to be thrilled with everything that is in your life? I am not asking this. But accepting, you will recall, is the *absence of the negative*—you do not reject, deny, or harbor hostile feelings toward something or someone. This is a major step forward and my aim in writing this important chapter.

Accepting your parents

I don't want to be insensitive or unfair here. There will be readers who will find this item perhaps the hardest of all to take. I need also to admit that I did not have a deprived background. I have been most fortunate. I truly thank God for my parents with all their faults. Some readers have grown up without a father or mother; some were rejected by one or both parents, some sexually abused, some physically battered, some emotionally bruised, and some with a father who was never around. The list is endless. I think of someone like Joyce Meyer, the international television preacher, who has stated publicly many times over how her own father abused her throughout her entire life at home, but who has turned trauma and tragedy into a legend. I would encourage anybody reading these lines to know that if you too can accept the teaching of this book generally and this chapter particularly, you also can turn into a legend right where you are. It is up to you. All things *do* work together for good to those who *love God*, not to those who hate Him for what He has allowed.

Do not forget that God chose your parents. He did. He did not make a mistake. I realize that what I am asking some to do seems far-fetched and out of the realm of realistic possibility, but I am now asking you to look to your heavenly Father and pray something like this:

Dear heavenly Father,
I believe You chose my parents, although I don't understand this; I affirm You as my Creator and Redeemer and ask You to help me see how all this can work together for good. Amen.

If you will keep repeating this and walk in all the light God puts in your path, you will one day see the wisdom of your heavenly Father in doing exactly what He did.

In the meantime, forgive your parents for all their mistakes— and forgive them totally. This is where to begin. Do this first, and the next step will be easier. To summarize:

1. Forgive them.
2. Accept them as God's choice of parents for you.
3. Don't look back.

Accepting the hard things you endured not only as you grew up but also since

This therefore refers to childhood memories but also to what happened as you grew older and became an adult. God allowed *everything* that happened to you, which He could have stopped but didn't. Why? I don't know. What I *do* know is that once a person becomes a member of the family of God, he or she has an incredible fringe benefit that no person outside the family has, namely, that one day you will be able to thank God for it all! I promise it! God does not promise to make everything work together for good for those outside the family. The promise is to those within the family. They and they alone get the benefit of the promise of Romans 8:28, the most quoted verse in this book:

> And we know that all things work together for good to them that love God, to them who are the called according to his purpose.
>
> —KJV

I shall end this book with a simple exposition of this magnificent verse.

What I am asking you to do is to accept, not reject, what God has allowed. And don't live in denial. Don't repress. You cannot accept yourself when at the same time you pretend certain things did not happen to you—the evil things—from peers, enemies, teachers, friends, and mentors.

In recent years I have had to bless the memory of a woman called Junka Smith. Yes, that was her real first name (but I changed the surname). She was my first schoolteacher in 1941. I was six years old at Crabbe Elementary School in Ashland, Kentucky. For some reason, she did not like me. And when I was asked by her to read aloud this line in front of a laughing class, "See Alice run," I got the words wrong and she stood behind me and shook my shoulders seemingly endlessly and certainly unmercifully—many times. I have had difficulty in reading ever since. For my wife, Louise, reading is fun; for me it is treacherous work. Yes, I am telling you the truth. And imagine what it was like when I came to England to "read for a degree," which I did. But it wasn't easy. But God permitted my first teacher to scare me to death by my getting words mixed up when reading aloud. I have a thought as to what His purpose was. I only know that God permits what can turn out for good. In my case, I believe it did. But I still find reading less exciting than fishing. You ask, "Have you actually blessed Junka Smith when you know she died over fifty years ago?" Yes. I needed to do that, even though she would not get the benefit of my blessing—but I got it.

Accepting your calling

Calling has many possible definitions, but here I refer to one's calling in life or career. Your calling may be lackluster, low profile, and relatively insignificant, or it may be exciting and regarded as in the limelight. But it is important that you accept your calling. Dr. Clyde Narramore says that your abilities are God's hint as to what you should do in life. C. H. Spurgeon used to say, "If God calls a man to preach He will give him a pair of lungs." Accepting your calling may not be easy, especially if it does not lead you to a life of ease or glory. Paul said, referring to whether one was married or single, circumcised or uncircumcised, slave or free, "Each one should remain in the situation which he was in when God called him." He then added, as if correcting himself, "If you can gain your freedom, do so" (1 Cor. 7:20–21). Later on, dealing with the gifts of the Holy Spirit, he said much the same thing; although the gifts are by God's sovereign will (1 Cor. 12:11), one should "eagerly desire the greater gifts" (1 Cor. 12:31). We therefore have a loophole if we are not entirely happy with our situation.

But there comes a time when you *know that you know* God has put you in a particular place, and you have to stay with it. It could be your job at the moment. In my book *The Thorn in the Flesh* I listed one's unhappy employment as a possible thorn that God has allowed. You may be called to the mission field—and hate it. Some will say that if God calls you to a particular place He will also give you the desire. I answer: Sometimes. Not always. David Brainerd (1718–1747) was a missionary to people in the wilderness in upstate New York. He is regarded as a man most saintly indeed. But his biographer personally told me that Brainerd did not enjoy what he was called to do. It took careful, unbiased research to reveal this, looking at unpublished letters and conversations he had with others. It makes me admire Brainerd all the more! Sometimes we are called to do a job we don't like. If so, we are to accept it. Jesus turned His back on the glory He had with the Father in order to become a man, and you and I are required to be like that (Phil. 2:5). In my case, we came to the Florida Keys to retire and fish. My "retirement" is the joke of the century! I've never worked so hard in all my life, and I don't like it. We are so seldom at home. But I am not my own.

Accepting your sexuality

I have more to say about this in *The Thorn in the Flesh* in the chapter called "A Sexual Misgiving." A great number of Christians worry about sex and their own sexuality. A sexual misgiving is a feeling of doubt, fear, or lack of confidence about one's own sexuality or lack of sexual identity. There are basically three possibilities:

1. Having a desire for the opposite sex (heterosexual)
2. Having a desire for the same sex (homosexual)
3. Having no strong sexual feeling either way (asexual)

Heterosexual men have fears that range from doubts about masculinity and virility to unease about intimacy with the opposite sex. This falls into the category of pseudoguilt. Likewise, some women as well as men feel there is something wrong with them if they are not interested in sex. This too is pseudoguilt. Those who are attracted to the same sex often suffer enormous guilt over their sexual orientation. This is pseudoguilt *unless* one practices it—which makes it true guilt, because homosexual practice is sin.

As for feeling guilty because of having a homosexual proclivity, this is understandable. After all, whether one likes it or not, the Bible clearly indicates that homosexuality is unnatural (Rom. 1:26–27) and the practice is sinful (1 Cor. 6:9–11; Lev. 20:13). But God does not regard a person as guilty before Him merely because of one's sexual orientation or temptations. It is only when one gives in to temptation—whether it be heterosexual or homosexual—that one is guilty before God. I go into detail in my book *Is God for the Homosexual?* (The answer, by the way, is yes.)

Being a Christian, generally speaking, in my opinion, has nothing to do with one's sexuality or orientation. Even those Christians who are very highly motivated indeed to please God in all of their ways often find that their orientation does not change. I know of stories of those whose sexual orientation changed when they were converted—or underwent therapy. I know of more stories of those who through the power of the Holy Spirit were able to resist temptation, regardless of their sexual orientation. I know of one Christian pastor who said he has prayed in tears "with all my heart every night of the year" to be delivered from his homosexual orientation. I wish it were otherwise, but one's sexuality usually does not change with one's conversion—or even being doubly dedicated to Christ.

What *does* change is the ability to resist temptation through the power of the Holy Spirit. I'm sorry, but whatever one's sexual orientation, he or she does not have to give in to temptation. There are robust heterosexual males who resist temptation to have sex outside of marriage every day of the year, year after year—resisting solely for the glory of God. There are also many gay people who do the same.

Accepting your sexuality without sinning is pleasing to God. God will never make you feel guilty for your particular sexual proclivity. Some Christians might, sadly; but God will not—ever. You probably cannot help it that you are like you are—whether you are heterosexual, homosexual, or asexual. You *can*, however, resist temptation for God's glory. You can also consider seeking the advice of a godly pastor or counselor who can bring your sexuality into perspective with God's promise and power to break the grip of sin and temptation and prevent you from falling into sin in this area again. And if you are asexual, do not feel guilty; believe me, if one is going to have a thorn in the flesh, that is the one to have.

But could I give this gentle, loving counsel to the gay person who reads these lines: do not boast that you are gay as some have been prone to do in recent times. Why do this? If you need to tell it, then tell your pastor or someone who will not tell anybody. But if you want everybody to know, all you do is put focus on your-self and possibly put temptation in another person's way. I would urge you to accept yourself quietly, because Jesus does. His accept-ing you as you are is what really matters. Accept His acceptance, and do not seek another's. God's sole approval should be your goal (John 5:44). If you are gay, you have an opportunity to bring great glory to God by your refusal to give in to temptation, and—I guar-antee it—His "well done" will be worth it all at the judgment seat of Christ (2 Cor. 5:10).

Accepting your singleness—at least for the moment

This advice was the godly counsel of the apostle Paul in 1 Corinthians 7, although he made allowances for those who were not able to follow it (v. 36). If your heart aches over your being single, especially when God said of us even *before* the Fall, "It is not good for the man to be alone" (Gen. 2:18), you have every right to petition Him day after day to bring a husband or wife into your life. I would encourage you to pray like this.

The reason for this section of the present chapter is to set you free *not to feel guilty* as long as you are single. Many people fear being single because of a stigma they feel some people impose on their being single. Most of us grew up being told that we would be married, have children, and live happily ever after. What people may or may not think should not govern your fears. If God has called you to be single, then accept it. If he has not called you to a lifetime of singleness, keep praying that the right person will come into your life. But do pray for the *right* one. There is something far worse than being unmarried, and that is being married unhappily. My dad used to pray that I would not fall in love with the wrong girl. God answered his prayer, and I pray He will answer yours. In the meantime, should you be single, accept it until God changes it.

Accepting that you cannot have children

This part too will not apply to everybody, but for those married couples who yearn for a child, the pain can be very great indeed. Couples around them who are having children right, left, and center make them feel all the worse. Such couples can also be highly insensitive, taking the ability to have children for granted. Couples who cannot have children often feel there is something wrong with them—not merely physiologically but spiritually; therefore, they feel guilt as a result. The guilt for some will be far, far greater if there was sin in their past that could have directly contributed to their inability to have a child. We are therefore back to forgiving ourselves. One must do this, perhaps by rereading what has preceded in this book, so that you can move on.

Do not forget: only God can give life. If He does not select you as an instrument of giving life, accept His wisdom. In the words of an old hymn we sang as I grew up, "Some day He'll make it plain to me."[2] For now, then, accept His sovereign will in this matter.

Accepting your intellectual limitations

There is probably not a single person, including Albert Einstein (if he were alive), who would not want a greater brain. The more intelligent or clever you are, you realize how little you know and how much wisdom you lack.

Let me say, first of all, intelligence and wisdom are not the same. I remember the words of Mrs. Martyn Lloyd-Jones to me one day, speaking of a highly brilliant politician (who was also prime minister): "clever, but not wise." Yes. People may think that a high dose of intelligence gives one wisdom. It does not. The beginning of wisdom is the fear of the Lord (Prov. 1:7), and there are absolutely no exceptions to this biblical principle.

Dr. Martyn Lloyd-Jones used to make the interesting distinction between being intellectual and intelligent. Some have great intellects to grasp mathematics, science, medicine, or philosophy, but they will sometimes be literally unintelligent. That also means that they lack what we call common sense. Dr. Lloyd-Jones used to say that a Cockney taxi driver in East London often has more intelligence than an Oxford don.

God gave you your brain. Accept it. Accept its possibilities. Accept its limitations. Don't boast over how smart or clever you are, because at the judgment seat of Christ we are all going to find out! A good reason for being fairly transparent here on Earth when it comes to objectivity about yourself is to keep you from big-time blushing at the judgment.

If God wanted you to be an Oxford professor, He would have given you a brain for that. If He hasn't given you such a brain, don't pretend to be so clever and bright. It is foolish and so very silly.

As for wisdom—ah, this is different! God does not promise to increase your IQ, but He does promise to increase your wisdom. (See James 1:5.) And the secret to greater wisdom is out: wisdom will come to you in proportion to your seeking to know His Word and His ways. You can't ask for more than that! As Moses was told, "As thy days, so shall thy strength be" (Deut. 33:25, KJV), so it is with the need for wisdom, knowledge, and intelligence when you are enjoying your inheritance in the kingdom of God. God will supply what is lacking—you will want for nothing.

Whatever job He has called you to do, whether to be an office manager, a bus driver, a physician, a lawyer, a teacher, or a housewife, God will give you the presence of mind that you need.

In the meantime, accept your mind and intellect as God's gift. Read all you can; learn all you can. But know that He will not promote you beyond the level of the competence He gave you—to prepare you for where you are now. Accept yourself.

Accepting the truth about your faults

I have a chapter in *The Thorn in the Flesh* called "Personality Problems." We all have them, because we all have our faults.

This does not mean you don't want to improve. But what if your particular thorn in the flesh should be a personality defect to keep you humble? God could do that. He wants to keep you from being conceited or admired too much (2 Cor. 12:7).

What are your faults? They are probably what two or three people are already thinking (possibly saying) about you—if only they had the courage to tell you. And if one of your faults is that you get your feelings hurt too easily, and they won't tell you, this might be a start in your own quest to have a measure of objectivity about yourself. Or do you talk too much? Do you dominate the conversation in the group? Do you only get interested in a topic if it is about you? Are you not able to accept criticism without being defensive?

Notice that I did not say "accepting your faults," but rather accepting the *truth* about your faults. It means admitting that what people are saying about you is true, promising to deal with them as best as you can, but then getting on with life without a load of guilt on your shoulders. When you accept the truth about yourself, it will almost certainly take the edge off of that particular defect. This is because you become alert to it and want to do something about it.

Accepting the truth about your faults therefore means that you will not let what has been true in the past bring you down into a clinical depression but rather awaken you to the need there is improvement called for. What is more, you would not have found out about it if God did not bring it to your attention—to give you hope! So if you discover a personality flaw in yourself, don't be defensive, and don't beat yourself black and blue; but thank the

Lord He is not finished with you yet. This is a giant leap forward in accepting yourself.

Accepting yourself with a disability or illness

One of the most natural feelings in the world for some is to feel guilty when they are ill. What is more, think about those who have a disability owing to an accident, especially if it was their fault. How would you like to spend the rest of your life in a wheelchair knowing that you fell asleep at the wheel of your car that crashed into the one in front of you?

There are some people who will never get well unless God miraculously intervenes. What do they have to look forward to? Have you thanked God lately that you are not like that? Do you take for granted that you have mobility? Do you thank God that you are not afflicted with an incurable disease? Do you thank God that you are not emotionally ill? We should look at every single illness or disability with the thought, "There, but for the grace of God, go I."

But I address *you* should this section be relevant in your case. First, if you are feeling guilty, I will suggest that you reread chapter 2, "False Guilt." Second, know that God does not want you to feel guilty for your condition. Third, don't feel sorry for yourself. Fourth, don't grumble. Finally, realize how brilliant your testimony will be when people around you find you so cheerful and dedicated to God. You have a unique opportunity to glorify God *because* you are in that situation.

I will never forget when I first met Joni Eareckson Tada. Meeting her brought me—literally—to tears. Not because I saw her in her wheelchair, but because she was so cheerful! It was amazing! I felt so ashamed, thinking how I have complained about so many small difficulties (compared to her plight), and she was radiant with the love of Jesus as I seldom have witnessed. She has been a quadriplegic for about thirty years. She told me that she would welcome being healed except she fears she would lose the kind of intimacy she now has with the Lord.

The best way, therefore, to accept yourself in an unchangeable physical condition is to develop such a love for Jesus Christ and the Holy Spirit that you know God is pleased with you like that. When we know He is pleased with us, it (to me) is the most wonderful feeling in the world. Know also that you won't have those limitations forever. All this will change when we get to heaven. Joni Eareckson Tada said she looks forward to dancing with Jesus when she gets to heaven! I say Jesus is looking forward to that as much as she is.

Accepting yourself when you are locked in a physical disability gives you an opportunity to bring glory to God that others simply don't have.

Accepting yourself in the light of the mistakes you have made

We have almost come full circle now, for this proposition relates to forgiving ourselves totally for our sinful past. I have dealt with this matter also in chapters 2 and 3.

Whether you are feeling guilty that you did not get the job you wanted (because you did not prepare adequately), the career you wanted (but you made the wrong choice of studies), the person you could have married (but jilted), the crime that landed you in prison, the infidelity that cost you your marriage, or the ministry you lost through lack of self-control, you have no good choice but to *accept yourself as things now are* and see what God will do with you. That is what God is calling you to do at this very moment.

When I preached on the life of David and came to the place where the prophet Nathan reprimanded him, telling him that the sword would never leave his house, I made the decision to stop the series there. I had been for a year and a half dealing with the life of David (from 1 Samuel 16 and into 2 Samuel 12), but I completely lost heart when I anticipated what was coming for David. I had no motivation to continue—and told my deacons so. But a couple of weeks later (during the time of our prayer and fasting at Westminster Chapel), the Holy Spirit clearly spoke to me. I was not prepared for it. His surprising if not stunning word to me came something like this: "So you are not going to preach on the remainder of the life of David because of his sin and failure and what he now had to look forward to? *Don't you know, RT, that is where most of your people are?*"

It hit me between the eyes. I told this to the deacons and shortly recommenced preaching on the life of David. I can tell you, those were the most precious months of the entire series. I will never forget it.

So what if you are like David? I can tell you also that God was with David right to the end. And it was during that period David developed a greater intimacy with God and wrote many of his psalms. God wasn't finished with David yet. And if sins and mistakes are crippling you at the moment, the same God who loved David also loves you—just as much.

John Newton, author of the famed song "Amazing Grace," was one day speaking to his close friend, the poet William Cowper, musing over 1 Corinthians 15:10: "But by the grace of God I am what I am." Newton said to him, "I am not what I ought to be. I am not what I want to be. I am not what I hope to be, but thank God I am not what I used to be." Anybody who follows Jesus Christ ought to be able to say that. We are all a work in progress.

The same God who has commanded you to forgive yourself now says, "Accept yourself."

CHAPTER 9

A LIFE SENTENCE

You need to persevere so that when you have done the will
of God, you will receive what he has promised.

—Hebrews 10:36

Never give in, never, never, never, never—in nothing, great
or small, large or petty—never give in except to convictions
of honour and good sense. Never yield to force; never yield
to the apparently overwhelming might of the enemy.

—Winston Churchill[1]

Every noble work is at first impossible.

—Thomas Carlyle[2]

Readers of *Total Forgiveness* may recall that we know we have
totally forgiven others when we:

1. Don't tell what they did to us
2. Don't let them fear us
3. Don't let them feel guilty
4. Let them save face

5. Protect them from their greatest fear
6. Make it a lifelong commitment
7. Pray for them to be blessed

It is impossible to know which of these seven propositions is the most important; they will vary in relevance from person to person. But the one issue that must never be underestimated is that total forgiveness is a lifelong commitment—a "life sentence"—which means you have to do it as long as you live.

As for forgiving others, many people hastily assume they have done it merely because they did it once! They feel better instantly and don't look back. What frequently happens and what so many often forget is that the devil will remind us two weeks or two months later what "they" did, and we unwittingly lapse back into the same old pattern. We are back to square one. This is one reason why people lose their joy.

It is a faulty doctrine of sanctification that can lead people into thinking they have "arrived" because they thought they had *once and for all* given their whole lives totally over to God. A good feeling often emerges when we know we have consecrated ourselves completely to God. The problem is, people too often forget that they have to *keep doing it*! The heart is so deceitful—incurable—says Jeremiah 17:9. We think we have done our duty because we did it *once*. Sadly, that is not good enough! Not even close! Totally forgiving others is something you have to keep on doing—again and again and again—as long as you live. I wish it weren't so!

So too, then, with totally forgiving ourselves; it is a life sentence. We have to keep forgiving ourselves as long as we live. Why? For basically two reasons:

1. Our imperfect and frail fleshly nature—we forget so easily

2. Our enemy, the devil, who never goes to sleep or stops accusing us of our past

The last thing I would want for you is that you should read the first eight chapters of this book—and even feel much better—only to lose this new freedom in a short period of time. It would be cruel of me to end the book without this chapter—even if you believe that you have totally forgiven yourself for the first time in your life. You and I have more work to do. I want you to have a *permanent* victory over the flesh and the devil. The euphoria one frequently gets by making a hard decision that was absolutely right will not last unless you keep it up.

One of the highlights of my twenty-five years at Westminster Chapel was having Billy Graham preach for me. It was the largest number of people (over two thousand) I had seen at the Chapel. Over eighty people walked forward to make a public profession. One of them, deeply moved by Billy Graham's comment—"when you die, you will die alone"—was motivated to walk out to the front. The man himself, plus everyone present who knew him, especially the man who personally invited him to come, was thrilled. But the joy didn't last. This man did not welcome the implications of receiving Jesus Christ as Savior and Lord. There was nothing wrong with anything Billy said or anything unfair about his appeal for people to come forward. It is simply a fact that not all who make a profession of faith are truly saved.

Totally forgiving yourself, therefore, is not something you do merely once—or twice.

As in forgiving others who have hurt you, you may have to do it (in your heart) several times a day at first, if not also for a good while after that. Forgiving yourself is no different. It is a life sentence, like some medicines people must take in order to live longer or at least to have a better quality of life. Hopefully, then, totally forgiving yourself will become a part of your habitual thinking and also become easier and easier to do.

But you will always have to do it. We all do. We are "frail children of dust, and feeble as frail,"[3] as a hymn writer put it, and you have a ruthless enemy who knows every bad thing you have ever done and knows particularly what is likely to bring you down. I pray therefore that what you have learned in this book will be applied by your forgiving yourself for your past—as may become necessary again and again.

Do not forget the three Rs of spiritual warfare: recognize, refuse, and resist. I hope this book has also made a small contribution in helping you to recognize when it is Satan and not God at work. Once you *recognize* the enemy exploiting either your pseudoguilt or telling you that your sins are too horrible for the blood of Christ to wash away, *refuse him*! Do not give him any dignity by letting him succeed in the slightest manner. This means that you must refuse to dwell on any thought the devil puts into your head. That is where *resistance* comes in—you *keep* refusing. When the devil sees that you are not going to be influenced by his evil suggestion, he will flee. That is a guarantee (James 4:8; 1 Pet. 5:8).

But he may come back tomorrow. Be prepared for it. This is what you and I and tens of millions of other Christians are having to do until God calls us home to heaven.

WHAT IF YOU FALL?

You are not perfect. You are not glorified yet. As I have stated in this book, glorification, which means perfection and an end of all temptation and trial, will take place when Jesus comes again (1 John 3:3; Rom. 8:30). In the meantime you and I are going to slip and fall from time to time.

There are three levels of falling:

1. When you lapse back into not forgiving yourself

2. When you find yourself repeating the old habit that caused you to feel guilty in the first place

3. When you deliberately return to your old way of life

When you deliberately return to your old way of life

I choose to deal with the third proposition first: deliberately returning to your old way of life. I have one thing to say to you if you do this: you are a fool. You not only forfeit fellowship with the Father, the Son, and the Holy Spirit, but you also risk falling so as to be unable again to be restored to repentance (Heb. 6:4–6). Were that to happen, you will be irrevocably yesterday's man or woman. God will not use you again. God could take your life or, which I think is worse, let you live a long while on this planet in utter agony without there being any hope for you. You will be finished—like King Saul. Some of the saddest words in Holy Writ were uttered by King Saul:

> Surely I have acted like a fool and have erred greatly…and God has turned away from me. He no longer answers me, either by prophets or by dreams.
> —1 SAMUEL 26:21; 28:15

Whatever else is true, I plead with you as though I were on bended knee, don't be a fool. You may recall what John Newton said: "Thank God I am not what I used to be." If you become what you used to be, it is a choice you will have to live with in this life and in the age to come.

This third level of sinning, as I have chosen to put it, is absolutely unnecessary for you to fall into.

When you find yourself repeating the old habit that caused you to feel guilty in the first place

There may be far more than one sin, mistake, or failure in your past that could fit into this proposition. There *are* shades of gray here—not everything is black and white. Old habits die hard. First, remember that there is a difference between temptation and sin. Being tempted is not a sin—whether there are evil thoughts that come into your head or you say things that you regret: "We all stumble in many ways. If anyone is never at fault in what he says, he is a perfect man, able to keep his whole body in check" (James 3:2). And we aren't going to be perfect!

For example, I have vowed not to point the finger at anybody. Being judgmental is one of my greatest weaknesses. For this reason I personally read Luke 6:37, a verse I quoted in the Introduction of this book, every day (at least six days out of seven):

> Do not judge, and you will not be judged. Do not condemn, and you will not be condemned. Forgive, and you will be forgiven.

Why do I read it? Because, knowing I have this weakness, keeping it before me helps me not to repeat this sin so often. But I have to tell you, I still do it from time to time, I am ashamed to admit. But when I fall in this manner, I simply appeal to good old 1 John 1:9: "If we confess our sins, he is faithful and just and will forgive us our sins and purify us from all unrighteousness." I accept my forgiveness on the spot; I forgive myself, and I move on! This happens to me more than I care for you to know!

This second level of falling is, in my opinion, inevitable for every Christian. Expect this.

As for the failure that haunts me most—my lack of time with the children in days of yore—if I am not careful I could repeat this in some way, even now when one of our children phones and I am preoccupied and might reveal that I am too busy for them at the moment. This has happened. It is a grim reminder that there is still a lot inside me that is too like what I used to be. I therefore have to be very careful when this possibility comes along, or I will feel worse than ever. I still have to watch this.

The main thing I would underscore in this second level of repeating an old failure is the issue of whether it could bring shame upon Christ's name. If we are talking about scandalous sin, I would lovingly say to you: *avoid it as you would a dreaded contagious disease.* Don't get near it. The best way to keep from falling into sin is to avoid the temptation (Rom. 13:14). If, say, it is temptation to have sex outside of marriage, a questionable use of money, or abusing power you may have, fight the urge with all your might lest you cross over a line and find yourself in the third level I described above.

When you lapse back into not forgiving yourself

This is so easy to do. This is the main reason I have written this chapter. Totally forgiving yourself is something you will always have to do—always. I have already given the reasons for this, but let me add one more thing: learn to catch yourself by recognizing a sense of guilt coming on you. I did not say "sense of sin," because it is possible to have a sense of sin and know at the same time you are a forgiven person. In other words, you can have a sense of sin without feeling guilty all the time. You are simply aware of your utter debt to God and feel so unworthy in His presence.

A sense of guilt is different because guilt is painful. A sense of sin, knowing that Christ's blood has purified your sins, is not painful—that is what the cleansing blood of Jesus is for. But guilt hurts. When you find yourself hurting because of any failure in the past—recent or distant—remember that God did not put that feeling there. Remember too that what God did not put there does not deserve any dignity by your dwelling on it.

Rule of thumb: *catch yourself* when a guilty feeling comes on you, and reject it by refusing to think about it. This is almost certainly pseudoguilt at work, but keep in mind that pseudoguilt can become true guilt if you let it govern you. Never be governed by pseudoguilt. God does not want you to do that—Satan does.

THE OLD CHECKLIST

The seven principles from *Total Forgiveness*—listed in the first paragraph of this chapter—are appropriate here. Those very same seven tests by which you may know whether you have totally forgiven others are also the way by which you can gauge whether you have totally forgiven yourself.

1. *You must not talk about your old failure.* As you prove you have totally forgiven your enemies and those who have mistreated you by telling nobody what they did, so likewise you must not talk about your old sins. Not even to yourself! Don't let your mind have conversations with yourself or tell others what you have had to forgive yourself for. I have sometimes wondered if there are those who give their testimonies of what they have been saved from talk so much about their old life that they still yearn for it a bit! One suspects they enjoy talking about their old sins! In any case, don't talk about your past failure. It focuses on yourself and gives the enemy an opportunity to bring you down. You may need to tell one other person for therapeutic

reasons. This could be important for you. But don't keep talking about this to others. It does not help.

I have referred to my own sense of guilt only for one reason—hopefully that it would encourage you to know that I too have needed to forgive myself. In my own private world, however, I have refused to dwell on it; I have accepted my forgiveness from God and have pronounced myself *forgiven!*

2. *Don't give in to any sense of fear.* As totally forgiving others will mean you won't let them be afraid of you, so too don't let yourself be afraid—for any reason! This kind of fear is of the devil. Not totally forgiving yourself will be an unwitting beckoning of Satan to move in on you. He loves to spread fear—it is what he does. Don't forget these wonderful words: "God hath not given us the spirit of fear; but of power, and of love, and of a sound mind" (2 Tim. 1:7, KJV). The spirit of fear is more than timidity; it is like a virus, an aura of poison, that can sometimes be supernatural—as if the breath of Satan. Learn to recognize this fear *as soon as it creeps in*, and refuse to let it bring you down.

When you feel afraid, turn to the Bible. If fear comes on you in the night, quote Scripture. If that doesn't work, start thanking God for anything and everything you can think of! If that doesn't work, start singing. Have an old hymnal or modern songbook nearby. Or read a good book. Or watch a wholesome television program (if you can find one). *Do anything* that gets your mind off what the devil has injected into your head. When you realize God did not put it there, don't give the devil one inch.

3. *Don't accept any guilt over what you have confessed to God.* As forgiving others is not letting those who hurt you feel guilty but helping them instead to forgive themselves (as Joseph did with his brothers in Genesis 45:5), so you must learn to reject any guilty feeling that comes your way. You have confessed your sins to God. Show *Him* you accept His forgiveness by refusing to feel the slightest bit guilty for what is now under the precious blood of Jesus Christ.

As Joseph asked his brothers not to be angry with themselves for what they did, you too should send yourself the same message: do not be angry with yourself. Affirm the blood of Jesus by refusing to chastise yourself for your past. Imposing guilt on ourselves has a strange way of trying to atone for our past, which is competing with Christ's atonement. We feel we must "pay" by feeling guilty; it seems too unfair that we should not continue to feel bad for what we did. God says, "Stop it! Won't My removing the guilt through My Son's blood be enough for you? Therefore, stop feeling guilty!"

4. *Hold your head high as if you had never sinned and therefore have nothing to be ashamed of.* You may recall that Joseph let his brothers *save face* for what they did: "God sent me ahead of you to preserve for you a remnant on earth....So then, it was not you who sent me here, but God" (Gen. 45:7–8). Joseph made it easy for them to forgive themselves, stressing to them that God Himself was behind the whole thing! "When you let another save face—protecting their fragile ego

and self-esteem—you win a friend for life," said Dale Carnegie in *How to Win Friends and Influence People.*[4]

God now asks you not to look down on yourself as if you were a guilty criminal but to hold your head high, because He has been on your case all your life! Not only that; you are a coheir with Jesus Christ (Rom. 8:17)!

When a person is apprehended or arrested for a crime, you will often see them with a sack over their face or looking down rather than into the TV camera. They have lost face, at least for the moment. But God will not have a child of His who has been bought by His Son's blood looking like that! He therefore commands you to enjoy His forgiveness and know that He will make your past work together for good *as if* the whole thing—including your failure—were His own idea. That is the way God lets us save face, and He now asks you to treat yourself to His delicious forgiveness.

5. *Know that God wants no further embarrassment to come your way.* As Joseph protected his brothers from their darkest secret and ensured that their father Jacob would never know the truth of their heinous sin, you too should understand that God does not want you to worry anymore about more shame coming your way. We all have skeletons in the cupboard—every one of us. God gets no joy in exposing our past secrets, and He wants you to know that He does not wish to embarrass you.

"The truth is worse than what they know," David Pawson once said to my friend Rob Parsons in one of Rob's darkest hours. That is true of all of us. The whole truth will not be known, however, because God is determined to make it easy for us to move ahead without the nagging fear of the past lurking at our heels. What is more, God lovingly and mercifully shields us from the sight of how black and depraved we are. I suspect it would snap our minds in an instant were we to see all at once what we are totally like.

6. *Totally forgiving yourself is what you will have to do from now on.* The brilliance of Joseph lay in the fact that he genuinely and honestly totally forgave his brothers for what they did. The proof of this is that he *kept it up* after Jacob died. The brothers feared that Joseph would get vengeance on them in the end, but Joseph assured them that his forgiveness was absolutely real and permanent. Seventeen years after he first disclosed his forgiveness for what they did, he renewed his love for them (Gen. 50:19–21).

   You and I are to do the same thing with ourselves— forgiving ourselves again and again and again. Why? Because you can expect fresh challenges. You can expect the devil to use a different tactic—to catch you off guard. You keep resisting him. Never, never, never, never give in to the seemingly overwhelming might of the enemy!

7. *You must boldly and unashamedly ask God to bless you even though you know you don't deserve it.* As Jesus prayed for His enemies and persecutors who were as undeserving as any group of men that ever lived (Luke 23:34), so you should without any blushing ask God to bless *you.* You ask, "How can I ask God to bless *me?*

I have been so awful." I reply: because He wants to bless you. Don't deprive Him of doing what He longs to do. It does not bless Him when you let your unworthiness govern your prayer list. We are *all* unworthy. This includes both the highest-profile believers in the Bible and all those in the whole of church history.

"In every saint there is something reprehensible," said John Calvin. There is not a saint in the history of redemption who would not die a thousand deaths (if alive) were *all* about them to be revealed before the world. Join the club! And enjoy total forgiveness for all you have done by totally forgiving yourself.

But it is something you will have to keep doing. Get used to it. But the time will come when it is a little bit easier to do because God will help you to do it. The proof? He gave us what is arguably the greatest promise in the Bible: Romans 8:28.

CHAPTER 10

THE FAMILY SECRET

Broken wings take time to mend
Before they learn to fly again
On the breath of God they'll soar
They'll be stronger than before.

—Janny Grein[1]

And we know that all things work together for good to them that love God, to them who are the called according to his purpose.

—Romans 8:28, KJV

And we know that all that happens to us is working for our good if we love God and are fitting into his plans.

—Romans 8:28, TLB

Moreover we know that to those who love God, who are called according to his plan, everything that happens fits into a pattern for good.

—Romans 8:28, Phillips

And we know that in all things God works for the good of those who love him, who have been called according to his purpose.

—ROMANS 8:28

R omans 8:28 is the verse I write under my name when I sign a letter or a book for someone. It has been my greatest guiding comfort as far back as I can remember. I honestly don't know what I would do without this incredibly encouraging verse.

I have written this book for one reason: to make it as easy as possible for you to forgive yourself. I have also tried to write in such a manner that each chapter stands by itself, that is, by your reading any chapter, even without following the order I have chosen, you would be helped to forgive yourself.

I have come to the end of the book. I have asked, what if all I have said up to now has not worked for some reader? What if *you*, for example, have read every chapter but are still unable to forgive yourself? If I knew what question you may have that I have not answered, I would try to answer it here! So I ask myself, what is left out that I could say that might enable you to cross over the line between not forgiving yourself and totally forgiving yourself?

I can think of one thing: assuming you believe the Bible, that if Romans 8:28 were unfolded before your eyes and you would accept the literal truth of it, you would be set free. I would even say that if you had not read this very book but completely believed Romans 8:28, you might not need my book at all! Why? Because Romans 8:28 is given to us precisely to help us never to feel guilty. It is a verse that deals with the *past*. Not the future, but only the past.

It refers to our entire past—our preconversion past and our postconversion past. It refers to all that happened to you before you were saved, but also to whatever has happened to you since you were saved. My own preconversion past would be from the time I was born until I was six years old! I can't remember anything bad during that time. But I can think of a *lot* of sins and failures and folly in the last sixty-five years. I am so glad that Romans 8:28 covers the whole of our lives as it did with King David, whose sin ranks with the worst but which events God determined to work together for good in the end. What God did with David He does with all those who are members of the family of God.

I call it Paul's most extreme statement. Paul has made some stupendous claims in his epistles, among them:

1. Ungodly people are regarded as righteous the moment they put their faith in Jesus Christ (Rom. 4:5).

2. The Christian can overcome impossible odds: "I can do everything through [Christ] who gives me strength" (Phil. 4:13).

3. Those who give generously and cheerfully to the Lord will be made "rich in every way" (2 Cor. 9:11).

But when Paul said, "We know that in *all* things God works for the good of those who love him, who have been called according to his purpose," he put his pastoral, theological, and personal integrity on the line. Can you imagine the extraordinary, awkward, and even extreme situations that one of his readers might throw up to him and say, "Am I to believe that *this*...could work together for good?"

In the same way, I will ask you to think for a moment. Call to mind your most difficult moment. Your most shameful. The hardest to understand. When you were at your worst. When the greatest injustice was thrust upon you. When you were involved in the most tragic accident—whether your fault or not. I could go on and on. Please think about this.

Romans 8:28 guarantees to every person who loves God and is among the called according to His purpose that anything and everything that was negative, wrong, or unfair that has happened to them will eventually turn out for *good*. Why does God give us this promise? Two reasons:

1. Because it is true
2. Because He does not want you to feel guilty about the past

He wants you to believe that all will turn out for good. If you really believe that, you will feel less guilty; and when you know that God Himself wants you to believe that, I would have thought you are home! He says to you right now as you read these lines, "As for the past, leave it with Me. It is not your problem. It is My problem. It is My job to make all that has happened to you work together for good. It is what I do."

I can't be sure about you, but let me tell you what this verse does for me: it makes me feel *good*. Very good. And that is precisely the way God wants me to feel—and exactly the way He wants you to feel. Whatever is in your past—whether the skeleton in your closet or that difficult circumstance to understand—God takes the responsibility away from you and me in order to make it turn out for good.

So does Paul realize what he has said? I answer: yes. The verse is true even if Paul had not said it! His stating it is not what made it true. It was true already; therefore, he said it. I have translated this verse from the Greek, read many modern translations, and have debated this verse in public. What is often overlooked is that the context of Romans 8 would assume the truth of this verse even if Paul had not included it! As a matter of fact, he might not have included it! After all, it was not (to him) the high watermark of Romans 8. Paul was showing how those who have been adopted into the family of God are guaranteed the irrevocable and unchangeable love of God, that they will never be separated from that love. It is as though Paul said along the way, "Oh, by the way, let me add, we know that all things work together for good"—as if to fill in what could have been regarded as redundant. But he put it in. I am so glad he did!

This verse means literally that everything that has happened to us in our past—whether bad, evil, accidental, negative, sinful, or unjust—or the wrong things we have done, will *eventually* "work together" (all things coalescing in God's due time) for good. The phrase *work together* is a reference to "all things," not a reference to our working with God to make it happen. It is not I who determines whether all things work together for good; it is God who does it, just as it is God who ensures that we who are adopted into the family of God will never be disenfranchised from His family.

When I have quoted this verse over the years, there have been those who have said to me, "Sorry, but I simply do not believe that!" There are those who look at Paul's plain statement and say, "It ain't so." Why would they say this? It could be because they are not really in the family of God in the first place. After all, this is not a verse for the world. It is not a promise to those outside the family. Paul does not say that everything that happens to everybody turns out for good. He says it is applicable only for those in the family: those who love God and are called according to His purpose. Furthermore, only those *in* the family can believe it. It sounds too extraordinary for those outside the family. But it was not intended for those outside the family to believe! It is for *us*.

It is as though Paul is saying, "Others may not believe it, but *we* do." "You may not know it, but *we* know it." "The world may not know that all things work together for good for those who love God, but *we* know this." *We* know it. We who are in the family know this.

How do we know it? Because of two things. First, by experience. Paul has personally experienced the truth of this verse so many times that he uses a Greek word *oidamen,* which mainly means "knowledge of a well-known fact." It can therefore refer to one's personal experience. Paul discovered in his own life that every bad thing that happened to him turned out for good. Paul might have used the Greek word *ginosko,* a word that mainly refers to revealed or speculative knowledge. He doesn't use that word but uses a word that shows knowledge nobody should dispute, as if to say we know this as well as we know our name. In other words, there is knowledge in the public domain that people do not question: what goes up comes down; the distance from New York to London; rain and sun help plants grow. Nobody questions things like this. Paul therefore uses a word that, to him, is so appropriate that he states the *obvious*—that to those in the family there is a built-in fringe benefit: all things that happen to them work together for good!

I must tell you, I myself have discovered this thousands of times. I could write a whole book on Romans 8:28.

But there is a second reason Romans 8:28 is true, namely, the glory of God's Son is at stake. Paul discussed the matter of adoption. How is it that we can be called children of God? After all, God only had one "natural" Son—Jesus Christ, the God-man, who was man *as though* He were not God, and yet God *as though* He were not man. Jesus Christ was uniquely the Son of God. There could never be two, three, or millions. Only one, "God the One and Only" (John 1:18).

How, then, are we sons and daughters of God? By adoption. We have been chosen and placed into the family. That is not all; we have the same security in the family as Jesus Christ Himself has! We are called "co-heirs with Christ" (Rom. 8:17). That means that you and I are as secure in our position in the family as Jesus Christ Himself is in the Godhead. Jesus could never be thrown out of the Trinity! It is unthinkable. And yet that is how secure you and I are in the family of God.

For that reason, then, all that touches you and me touches Jesus—our elder brother! Whatever affects us affects Him. And when something bad happened to Jesus, the Father determined that it would work together for good! This is why Peter preached at Pentecost that Jesus was handed over to the Jews "by God's set purpose and foreknowledge; and you, with the help of wicked men, put him to death by nailing him to the cross. *But God raised him from the dead"* (Acts 2:23–24, emphasis added). If that is not causing evil to "work together for good," I don't know what is! The cross and the resurrection of Christ are a paradigm illustration of how all things work together for good to those who have been adopted into the family of God.

But not all believe this. It is the *family secret.* "We know," says Paul, we who are in the family. We have found it to be true but also discovered the reason it is true: God's honor is at stake!

Why, then, does Paul believe that all things work together for good to those who love God and are the called? As God made the evil done to Jesus work together for good, so those who are "in Christ" (a phrase Paul uses many times) have the same benefit. The crucifixion was the most evil act that was ever committed, but the resurrection of Jesus turned the death of Jesus into the greatest thing that ever happened!

That is the security *you* have.

"But," you will say, "Jesus never sinned. My problem with guilt is my sinful past."

I answer: the blood of Jesus put away your sin as though there were no sin left to be found. God promised to "tread our sins underfoot and hurl all our iniquities into the depths of the sea" (Mic. 7:19). In other words, your sins cannot be found!

Did you ever notice the genealogies in Matthew 1? They show the bloodline of God's Messiah, our Lord Jesus Christ. You will recall the wickedness of King David: he committed adultery and then murder to cover the adultery. It was an abominable sin. But here is the way it comes out in the end: "David was the father of Solomon, whose mother had been Uriah's wife" (Matt. 1:6). David had other wives that God could have chosen through whom His Son would be traced. God chose Bathsheba, the very woman with whom David committed adultery. Why? To demonstrate that He turns wickedness into good, so that in the genealogy of Jesus you might even think that what happened in David's life was the way it was supposed to be! God "covered" David's sin and determined to make it work together for good. That is what He will do with you!

A caution, however, is in order: *that something works together for good does not mean it was right at the time.*

Never forget this. Not all that happens is good. That it works together for good doesn't mean it was right. It was anything but right. Romans 8:28 does not say that all that happens is good. No. Romans 8:28 says that all things *work together*—they coalesce and come together in God's timing—for good.

That also means it takes time for the truth of this verse to be fulfilled in one's life.

One other caution: do not apply this verse to the future. Someone might foolishly say, "It doesn't matter what I do; it will work together for good." I reply: Do you want to go through what

David went through? Do you welcome God's rugged chastening in order to teach you a lesson?

Romans 8:28 is a verse that refers to our *past*, not the future. If you want to be a fool, try applying Romans 8:28 to what you plan to do that you know is wrong.

What the brothers did to Joseph was wrong. It would be many years before Joseph could say, "God intended it for good" (Gen. 50:20). Romans 8:28 is true, but it may not be carried out by tomorrow morning. It always takes time.

Romans 8:28, however, is not given to you that you wait to see its fulfillment before you can have the enjoyment of it. It is given as a promise. It is sealed by the blood of Jesus. God guarantees it to be fulfilled. You are to believe it now and enjoy it now—even if things at the moment don't appear to have worked together for good. God wants you to trace the rainbow through the rain *now* and enjoy knowing *now* that all that is in your past is safely in God's hands. He is the one who will make things work together for good.

In other words, don't try to hasten its fulfillment! Some people have erroneously translated Romans 8:28 to mean that God works together with people to make it happen. That means that if people don't adequately cooperate with God, Romans 8:28 won't be fulfilled. Whatever kind of promise is that? Listen! Romans 8:28 has the resurrection of Jesus Christ to back it up. What did *anybody* have to do with raising Jesus from the dead?

It is God who makes it happen. In fact, the NIV stresses this in its translation of Romans 8:28: "We know that in all things *God works* for the good of those who love him, who have been called according to his purpose" (emphasis added). Don't *you* try to make it happen; let God do it. Don't worry. He will. It is what He does and what He does best. It gives Him great pleasure to do this. Don't elbow in on His territory to hasten the fulfillment of Romans 8:28; you will only delay it.

One further clarification—already implied. This verse is true not only to those in the family but to those who also love God. It is possible that some of those in the family have fallen but have not yet been restored and hence don't love God at the moment. If you don't love God, don't expect Romans 8:28 to work for you. It works for those who "love" Him—not those who once loved Him. *Love* is in the present tense.

The "called according to his purpose" means those who have been adopted into the family. They have been effectually called by the Holy Spirit. It is not a word that those outside the family can apply. It is the family secret.

How good is "good"? *Good* is an adjective; there is good, better, and best. Would you be disappointed if you were told it won't turn out for the "better" or the "best"?

Not to worry. Nobody gets the best in this life. God's best, if that is the way to put it, was in the Garden of Eden before the Fall. Adam and Eve took care of that for all of us. This is why you and I were born into a fallen world; we inherited the sin of our first parents.

But Jesus Christ is the Lamb that was slain from the foundation of the world (1 Pet. 1:19–20). The fall of our parents in the Garden of Eden hardly took God by surprise. What they did was anticipated from the beginning of Creation.

However, when God created the world and then took a look at what He made, He saw that it was "good" (Gen. 1:25). That was *before* the Fall. If God can call His creation good before the Fall, then give a promise thousands of years later to His redeemed, fallen creatures, that ensures "good" to them, I can only say: what God calls good is good enough for me. What is more, God wants to vindicate the blood of His Son so that fallen creatures who have the benefit of that blood are given a dignity that is at least equal to, if not grander than, the loveliness of creation before the Fall.

So if God calls His prefallen creation "good" and promises to His redeemed people that all will turn out for "good," then God's good is good enough for me.

I close the book with some of the words from one of the most moving modern hymns I have come across. It came into our lives when Louise first heard Janny Grein sing the lovely hymn she wrote a few years ago. Janny visited Westminster Chapel and sang it for all of us there. It is called "Stronger Than Before":[2]

> As the seasons make their turn
> There's a lesson here to learn
> Broken wings take time to mend
> Before they learn to fly again
> On the breath of God they'll soar
> They'll be stronger than before
>
> Don't look back into the past
> What was fire now is ash
> Let it all be dead and gone
> The time is now for movin' on.

INTRODUCTION

1. Alexander Pope, *Essay on Criticism*, part ii, line 15, as quoted at http://www.bartleby.com/100/230.99.html (accessed April 13, 2007).

2. Monergism.com, "St. Augustine of Hippo," http://www.monergism .com/thethreshold/articles/augustine.html (accessed April 13, 2007).

CHAPTER TWO
FALSE GUILT

1. Paul Tournier, *Guilt and Grace* (New York: HarperCollins Publishers, 1982).

3. The Quotations Page, "Quotations by Author: Henry Kissinger (1923–)," http://www.quotationspage.com/quotes/Henry_Kissinger/ (accessed May 22, 2007).

CHAPTER THREE
TRUE GUILT

1. BrainyQuote.com, "Francis Schaeffer Quotes," http://www .brainyquote.com/quotes/quotes/f/francissch192586.html (accessed April 12, 2007).

2. W. C. Crain, *Theories of Development* (Upper Saddle River, NJ: Prentice-Hall, 1985), 118–136, as quoted at Pacific Lutheran Theological Seminary faculty pages, http://faculty.plts.edu/gpence/ html/kohlberg.htm (accessed April 12, 2007).

3. "Come Thou Fount" by Robert Robinson and John Wyeth, public domain.

4. "Trust and Obey" by John Henry Sammis and Daniel B. Towner, public domain.

CHAPTER FOUR
GUILT, GRIEF, REGRET, AND REPENTANCE

1. William Shakespeare, *Much Ado About Nothing*, 3.2. Reference is to act and scene.

2. The Samuel Johnson Sound Byte Page, "London Quotes," http://www.samueljohnson.com/tiredlon.html (accessed April 12, 2007).

CHAPTER FIVE
OUR TWIN SINS

1. Interview in *The Sunday Telegraph,* as quoted at J. John and Mark Stibbe, *A Box of Delights* (London: Monarch Books, 2001), 53.

2. John Piper, *Desiring God* (Colorado Springs: Multnomah Publishers, Inc., 1986), 222.

3. "It Is a Thing Most Wonderful" by William Walsham How, public domain.

CHAPTER SIX
OUR GREAT ACCUSER: THE DEVIL

1. "A Mighty Fortress Is Our God" by Martin Luther, public domain.

2. "Approach My Soul the Mercy Seat" by John Newton, public domain.

3. "The Solid Rock" by Edward Mote and William Bradbury, public domain.

CHAPTER SEVEN
SPIRITUAL GIANTS

1. Robert Burns, "To a Louse," 1785, as quoted at the World of Robert Burns, "Critical Analysis of To a Louse," http://www.robertburns .plus.com/louse.htm (accessed March 8, 2007).

CHAPTER EIGHT
ACCEPTING OURSELVES

1. Rick Warren, *The Purpose Driven Life* (Grand Rapids, MI: Zondervan Publishing Company, 2002).

2. "Some Day He'll Make It Plain" by Lydia S. Leech, public domain.

CHAPTER NINE
A LIFE SENTENCE

1. The Churchill Centre, "Never Give in, Never, Never, Never," http://www.winstonchurchill.org/i4a/pages/index.cfm?pageid=423, (accessed March 13, 2007).

2. BrainyQuote.com, "Thomas Carlyle Quotes," http://www .brainyquote.com/quotes/authors/t/thomas_carlyle.html (accessed March 16, 2007).

3. "O Worship the King" by William Kethe, Johann Michael Haydn, Robert Grant, William Gardiner, 1486, public domain.

4. Dale Carnegie, *How to Win Friends and Influence People* (N.p.: Pocket, 1998).

CHAPTER TEN
THE FAMILY SECRET

1. "Stronger Than Before" by Janny Grein, as quoted at Broken Wings Ministry, "Theme," http://www.brokenwings.org/Theme/theme.html (accessed March 15, 2007). Used by permission.

2. Ibid.

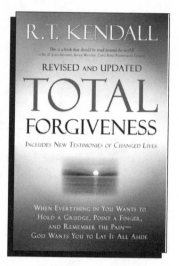
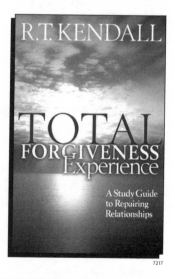

FREE NEWSLETTERS
TO HELP EMPOWER YOUR LIFE

Why subscribe today?

☐ **DELIVERED DIRECTLY TO YOU.** All you have to do is open your inbox and read.

☐ **EXCLUSIVE CONTENT.** We cover the news overlooked by the mainstream press.

☐ **STAY CURRENT.** Find the latest court rulings, revivals, and cultural trends.

☐ **UPDATE OTHERS.** Easy to forward to friends and family with the click of your mouse.

CHOOSE THE E-NEWSLETTER THAT INTERESTS YOU MOST:

- Christian news
- Daily devotionals
- Spiritual empowerment
- And much, much more

SIGN UP AT: **http://freenewsletters.charismamag.com**

8178